# Connecting Caregivers

# Connecting Caregivers

## Answers to the Questions You Didn't Know You Needed to Ask

### Expert Advice, Practical Tools and Personal Stories

Linda Burhans, Editor

ISBN   978-0-9975849-0-5
ISBN   978-0-9975849-1-2 (e-book)
Library of Congress Control Number:  2016908133

Skylar Thomas Publishing Inc.
P.O. Box 4462
Seminole, FL 33775
727-365-8383

# Dedication

With a full heart I dedicate this book to my
"wicked stepmother," Heidi McCauley—my other mother,
friend, confidant, comrade, biggest cheerleader, and the best
caregiver in the world to my dad.
This book would not be possible without you.
I am so grateful for you.
With much love.

Also by Linda Burhans

Good Night and God Bless—
Celebrating Love, Laughter & the Lessons of Loss

To contact Linda, read her weekly blog, or locate other resources,
visit www.LindasCaregiverConnections.com

# Contents


Acknowledgments .................................................... i

What Will Be the Final Chapter?
*Marieke Van Donkersgoed* ........................................ 1

## Learning to Navigate

What Is Home Care?
*Jonathan Bowman* ............................................... 13

A Culture Change in the World of Aging
*Mel Coppola* .................................................... 22

Are You Part of the Sandwich Generation?
*Gary Joseph LeBlanc* ........................................... 33

What is a Certified Geriatric Care Manager or
Aging Life Care Specialist?
*Laura Freed* ................................................... 36

Creating a Family Caregiver's Home Health Emergency
Care Plan
*Linda Burhans* ................................................. 39

Are You Legally Prepared for Incapacity?
*Stephanie M. Edwards* .......................................... 42

How Do You Keep Your Financial Plan on an Even Keel?
*Candy Goodwin* ................................................. 49

What Is a Reverse Mortgage and How Does It Work?
*Malcolm Tennant* .......... 55

How Can I Access Veteran Benefits?
*Karyn Rizzo* .......... 65


## Learning to Cope

The Caregiver "AAA" Dilemma
*Linda Burhans* .......... 75

Optimal Mental Health for Caregivers
*Heidi Crockett* .......... 77

How a Little Boy Changed an Elderly Man's Life
*Linda Burhans* .......... 90

How Can Journal Writing and Support Groups
Help Me as a Caregiver?
*Mary Jane Cronin* .......... 92

Acknowledging Your Loved One's Feelings
*Linda Burhans* .......... 100

The Power of Story
*Paula Stahel* .......... 103

Have You Accepted the Things You Cannot Change
and Changed the Things You Can?
*Karen Karle-Truman, Ph.D.* .......... 111

Caregiver Clubhouse
*Linda Burhans* .......... 117


## Learning to Accept

Dementia Awareness
*Maria Winer* .......... 121

Mary & Aunt Bevie—When the Roles Reversed
*Linda Burhans* .......... 123

What Are the Signs and Symptoms of Dementia
and What Should I Do?
*Christine Varner* .................................................... 126

Purple Cities Alliance ............................................ 140

A Blast from the Past
*Linda Burhans* ...................................................... 141

How Can I Be Engaged with My Loved One?
*Carole Ware-McKenzie* .......................................... 143

Queen of the House
*Linda Burhans* ...................................................... 154

Is a Memory Care Community the Right Choice
for My Loved One?
*Rebecca Weitzel* .................................................... 157

What Does That Mean? A Guide to Caregiving Terms
*Dale Griffen* ......................................................... 165

Website Resources ................................................. 180

## Acknowledgments

When my mom decided to sell the big family house on Long Island and move near me in Florida, she was a vibrant woman of seventy-six. We looked forward to years of laughter and adventures, and plenty of visits from my two sisters and brother and other family escaping from cold winters up north. Then came news we didn't expect—cancer. Within two years Mom was gone.

What I also didn't expect was that becoming my mom's caregiver would radically alter my own life path. Like all caregivers, I was thrown into a role I wasn't prepared for. With every new challenge I had to search out answers without knowing where to start. And with every new challenge I met wonderful people who were generous in sharing knowledge and their own experiences.

After Mom died, I wrote a book, Good Night and God Bless, about our final journey together. When I was out promoting the book or speaking, every single time people came up to me in tears, looking for answers and help. Soon I was embarked on a new career path—connecting caregivers to each other, and helping them find answers to the questions they didn't even know they needed to ask. My passion and mission became assisting other caregivers with education, resources, and a shoulder to lean on.

And after facilitating more than 1200 support groups and speaking to many, many caregivers, my second mission is helping caregivers help their loved ones find some purpose in their own lives.

I always say that your caregiving experience can be the

most horrific time of your life or downright beautiful, depending on how you handle it. And how you handle it depends on having answers to the challenges you face.

I am grateful to all the people I have met—caregivers themselves, and those who help them. Most of all, I am grateful to the people who contributed to this book. Each of them is someone I know, like, trust, and can count on. A special thank you to Paula Stahel, editor extrodonaire. Your expertise, guidance, and sense of humor helped me keep my sanity and made this journey enjoyable. And I thank the community of professionals and other people who surround me, who really want to make a difference in the lives of caregivers.

*Linda Burhans*
*The Gal Who Cares for the Caregivers.*

*Marieke van Donkersgoed*

## What Will Be the Final Chapter?

There is a beautiful Gaelic term, Anam Cara, which means "soul friend." In the Celtic spiritual tradition, it refers to the understanding that we are spiritual beings in physical bodies, rather than merely physical beings. When you connect with another person and become completely open and trusting with that individual, your two souls, or spirits, begin to flow together. The Anam Cara is the person who is fully and truly present with someone in their final weeks and days of life, with pure acceptance of the other, holding them in wholeness, beauty, and light. You, as a caregiver, may be in the privileged position to become the soul friend of your beloved, in the final chapter of their life's journey.

This chapter is about more than my work as an end-of-life doula. This chapter is about my mission in life: to create better understanding and experience of dying and death nationwide. In America, we have become unfamiliar with and disconnected from death, which is the most unavoidable and natural phenomenon in all of our lives. So disconnected that we allow the dying process to happen in aloneness, under tube lighting behind curtains, and in fear. Only in this country has death become a medical event, far removed from its truth as a social and tribal happening. It has become the unspeakable, the biggest fear of many, while there is nothing to fear but the fear itself.

I received my calling when I was my mother's caregiver, during her four-and-a-half month process of dying from pancreatic cancer. She was a vital eighty-three-year old. Other than an occasional cold, she was never ill. Her diagnosis shook our world. The odds for a cure were against her, and she almost immediately decided to accept the fact and make the best of her time to come. Her wish was to die at home. I was able to fulfill that wish for her, by moving in and giving her my word that I would not leave before her. It became the most incredible learning experience of my life. I became my mother's Anam Cara.

The most profound lesson was that nothing I had believed about dying and death was true. Nothing I expected or dreaded happened. My mother was my teacher. Her acceptance of her human lot, her surrender to the process, her acceptance of my care, showed me that love surmounts all fears. Love eases pain. Love heals wounds. Love gives hope through death.

Love conquers death.

This chapter is about loving, comfort care. More than fourteen hundred years ago, long before there was such a thing as pain management through medication, the original "hospices" were situated along the trade routes and pilgrimage trails in Europe. Exhausted and sick travelers would find care and shelter in these first "places of hospitality," where compassionate monks and laymen offered food and rest. Often, the travelers would die in these places. They would be cared for and kept comfortable and clean. There would be someone present for them in the moment of death. It was a known fact that someone who was cared for and kept comfortable and clean had a good chance of a gentle death. Nothing has changed about that. Today, being present with and holding the dying in loving care and comfort is perhaps even more important than the medications to still physical pain.

As much as every person is unique, so is every death. Interestingly, it is often in the way someone lived that they die. People who were controlling during their lifetimes may want to be in control of the process and sometimes hold on more rigidly, or actually control the circumstances of their death. People who were more relaxed and surrendered during their lives often have a more relaxed way of surrendering into their final transition.

When someone is first confronted with impending death, enormous mental and emotional shifts take place, often long before there are any physical changes. There can be confusion, fear, and disbelief. A lot of the dynamics of this time are from pure grief. Shifting the mind from the process of living to the process of dying bears enormous consequences. We often think of grief as something we go through when we lose something or someone, but it is the dying who lose everything and everyone. It wasn't until I witnessed my mother's dying process that I realized that her grief over losing her children and grandchildren, her friends, her health, and her future, was many times the grief we each had for losing her!

Whether someone has been ill for a longer period of time or a diagnosis comes out of the blue, the actual fact of our mortality is tough to accept. When you are giving care to someone in the final stage of life, you are stepping into an unparalleled opportunity to witness life at its fullest. Dying well is work of the heart. It is fueled by love. Love between you and your dying loved one. It is hard, intense, and often exhausting work, but what a privileged place to be.

If and when your loved one is still ambulant, this is the time to go places and do things that are important for them, and to make more memories. Visiting people while good conversations can still be had offers great opportunity to let the news become reality, while also informing others and receiving comfort and support for the time to come. Openness about the situation is of huge value for all involved. Looking the situation in the eye and talking about it is empowering. It reveals anticipatory grief, which, if expressed and shared at this time, can really help with the grief process to come after the death. Being open about it also reveals uncertainties, fears, and questions to be answered. The more your beloved can share and express during this time, the more complete and meaningful this process will be for everyone.

Once there is openness and acceptance of the situation, then is the best time to address formal documents such as a Do Not Resuscitate Order, Living Will, Powers of Attorney, and other final wishes. This also was the time when my sister and I started talking with our mother about her ideas for her funeral. The information we got from her was invaluable in creating a beautiful celebration and send-off, with all the music she loved, the readings, the candles, and the rattan casket she preferred. Most importantly, it allowed my mother to be a part of her own goodbye ceremony, and her spirit was fully present when the time came.

Dying is the process of the physical body releasing the spirit. Where spirit came into human being, in the body, with the first breath at birth, it will leave the body and go back to spirit form with the last breath. This, itself, is not painful and those who die of old age usually will have no physical pain at all. If there is a disease, the disease can cause pain, and medication should be able to keep someone fully comfortable.

However, emotional and spiritual pain, caused by fear or unfinished business, can prolong the dying process and keep the spirit locked in the body. You, as the Anam Cara, can play an essential part in relieving these tensions. Your presence and ability to be open, and trusting of whatever it is that is keeping your loved one from relaxing, will allow them to speak their emotional and spiritual needs. For some, this may be the time to call in a clergy, hospice, or an end-of-life doula to provide guidance. It is very rewarding to lift these burdens and uplift the energy of your beloved.

Although every death is unique, there are dynamics to watch for, which will indicate where someone is in the process and what you can do to best assist. There is excellent literature available at the library and through hospice to use for guidance. Please note that when someone is dying of old age, these signs can show over a much longer period of time. When someone is in disease, you may notice that about six months to a month before death they start to turn inward, sleep more, and participate in fewer social situations. Don't be unnerved. It is all very normal. Preparing for death is a delicate and private affair, which demands focus and concentration on a level we seldom even touch during our lifetime. You are not being shut out. Your beloved is shutting himself or herself in, cocooning if you will, in preparation for the release of their spirit.

It is important to allow this to happen, but also to be attentive and alert when they are awake and aware. Ask your loved one what they are experiencing. If you have seen them "busy" in their sleep, ask if they remember what they were dreaming. Hold what they tell you in truth, even if it sounds fantastic and unbelievable. Who are we to know what is real and unreal until we ourselves die? These times can offer spectacular sharing and insights in the process, if you can gently be—just be—open to the experience without fear.

Sometimes the dreams will lead to subjects of "unfinished business," which may be important to address. Does someone need to be contacted? Do relationships need to be reconciled? Is there a desire to visit a favorite place or family member? Does a story need to be told? Being present, hearing these needs and wishes—and being helpful in fulfilling them, will make you an invaluable participant in the process.

In this phase also, the dying begin to lose their appetites for their usual foods and drinks, and ask to be left alone to rest or sleep rather than eat. If you have been taking care of someone for a long time, this may feel like rejection of your good care and you may want to stress harder to meet their needs. As a culture we relate wellbeing to food and offer it as a token of love. Offer it as you like, but don't force it if it isn't wanted. If you are used to preparing three meals a day at specific times, start offering smaller snack-like meals instead, which may not even be eaten. The body will need less fuel. Offer anything that is asked for, but don't force anything.

We often panic and send our dying to the hospital when they decline food because we fear their starving to death if we don't force them to eat. In the natural process, the first thing the body needs to do is decline calories. It no longer needs fuel to live while preparing to die. The needed intake changes from food to love and encouragement. The love and encouragement provided by the Anam Cara, which is to simply be fully present and allow the process to be what it will be, to love the person, to care for them while allowing all that is, and honoring the process.

While still functioning quite normally physically, the soul is starting to take the lead in the process to come. Even when the mind hasn't yet accepted impending death, the soul is aware and is doing what it needs to, in preparation to leave the body. It is often a clearly recognizable change, if you can be in awareness of what you are witnessing.

There will come a time when your loved one is less out of bed than in it. If at home, when their world becomes as small as the bedroom or a bed in the living room, it is helpful to make some changes in their direct surroundings. Placing the bed so the person in it can see out the window retains a connection to the world outside. Being aware of daytime and nighttime creates a sense of stability in the rhythms of time, while birds on the feeder or a squirrel in a tree can become objects of intense joy. Placing one or more comfortable chairs close by will make it easier for visitors to relax and feel comfortable as well.

When comfort care is offered—through hospice or you, at home or in the hospital—it is time to make the person more important than their condition. Put medical items out of sight if possible and replace them with your loved one's favorite objects. Soft lighting options, for the hours when physical care is not provided, are relaxing for everyone. Perhaps tape some photographs of favorite people and places on the walls. Ask children or grandchildren to be creative and bring drawings. I find it so strange that the usual place to hang cards and drawings is above the patient in a hospital bed. Pin well wishes to the draperies and opposite walls, so your beloved can see them. Flowers bring a joyful touch. Scented candles or plug-in air fresheners can offer calming aromas and dampen unwanted odors around the deathbed. A simple CD player with relaxing music can soften the unpleasant sounds of labored breathing or silence. There are so many little things we can do to create a lighter energy in the space.

The natural dying process is very predictable. The body is in agreement with the soul on the timing of slowing down and shutting down the functions and organs. If left alone, it is usually a gentle and painless process, too. Unfortunately, fear of the impending loss often drives caregivers and well-meaning bystanders to interfere with this process.

Interfering with the natural process by tubing, hydrating, ventilating, and testing for a final possible miracle creates unnecessary physical suffering. The body becomes "confused." A body receiving nutrition when organs can no longer process it will react counter-productively. Hydrating a body with shut down kidneys will also be counterproductive. Suffering can be avoided in so many ways if we can stay in a place of love and acceptance rather than fear. Be present in the process, talk it through with your beloved, and realize all is happening in perfect order.

When the silences become longer and the conversations shorter, pay good attention to what your loved one says. Sometimes their language can be very symbolic. Stating they "want to go home" when they are home, or "I have to pack my suitcase," can mean they are preparing for their final journey. They may seem less clear and more disoriented in their waking time too. Don't be alarmed. Their focus is on their inner work now, and they will easily and peacefully slide back out. When my mother went through this time and I was uncertain of what to do for her, she said, in a lucid moment: "Just be there. I like to know you are sitting there reading your book." She just wanted my presence, nothing more, nothing less.

Your loved one's sleep may become very deep, with head tilted back and mouth open. Breathing can come with soft moaning or gurgling. Their hands may reach out, as if there is someone or something for them to touch or grasp. Or they may anxiously pluck at the bedding with busy hands. A gentle and comforting hand-stroke across the head or cheek may seem to go completely unnoticed. Do it anyway. Your presence is important and felt on a very deep level. Your soft, encouraging words will help you stay focused and present as well.

You can create a magical energy around you and your beloved. This is the time when your role as Anam Cara is almost palpable. Time and space, as you know it, change. Days flow into the next. The world outside is what it is, while you focus on and breathe with your loved one.

Very near to death, the dying will often speak of visions

they have of people who have long passed. They sometimes lay with open eyes and gaze into a corner of the room intensely, as if aware of presences we cannot see. Weeks before she passed, my mother saw her deceased sister by her bedside. She also saw waving fields of wheat-like crops in a color of green that she couldn't compare to any green she had seen before. Some people describe seeing angels, or sometimes even Jesus. I have never experienced a dying person to be upset by these experiences, not even the ones who described themselves as not being spiritual. Usually there is a sense of surprise and joy. It seems comforting to the dying to know these spirits and loved ones are there for their support and to welcome them on the other side. It seems completely normal to them, so it helps if you accept it as normal too. It seems as if the soul begins to "step out" of the body in the weeks and days before the actual passing. Perhaps it is part of preparation for the final departure, perhaps it is to take a peek in the next dimension.

Your loved one will most likely become less and less responsive, until they slide into a coma-like state three weeks to one week before death. Their labor—the "birthing process" from this life—has begun.

If you become well informed about the process of active dying, you will be less afraid of what you are seeing. You may actually know to look for the signs indicating where your loved one is in the process, to be aware of how you can be of assistance.

Dying is not a medical affair. Dying does not require medical professionals. Like a mother during childbirth, which requires many similar energies, a dying person needs support and guidance. A stress-free space and surroundings prepared for the process, as well as a well prepared and fearless soul friend, can make for a good death without suffering.

I remember my mother's final minutes with fondness

rather than sadness. We were so well prepared. When her time came, she had been barely responsive for two days. My sister and I took turns holding vigil and we had begun to breathe as she breathed. Our world followed the rhythm of her being. We were totally focused, not knowing what to expect. Then suddenly her breathing changed and she seemed to want to communicate with us. We slid into position on both sides of her bed, close to her head, our nearness creating gentle pressure on her body, and whispered softly, "Mama, are you ready?"

Her breath rapid, she answered in her native tongue, "Yah."

We told her we loved her and how well she did. How proud we were of her and how we would miss her. She was listening intently. We thanked her for being our mother, and told her it was okay to go. We would be okay. In her Dutch language we said, "Dag, lieve Mama"—bye, sweet Mama, and she answered, "Dah." Then, with one last deep breath, her spirit left her body. It was the most rewarding and loving experience I ever had in my life. I will never forget it.

I wish for all who are caring for their dying loved ones to have experiences like mine. I hope you will realize how much of it is in your power. Love is the fuel of dying. Loving someone and being prepared to be their Anam Cara will eliminate the fear and suffering. It is so.

*Marieke van Donkersgoed is a non-medical end-of-life care specialist, certified holistic life coach, death doula (servant to the dying), and educator. Her work is focused on the mental, emotional, and spiritual dynamics of aging, dying, and grief. Through Cypress Healing, Marieke works with clients at home, and with care organizations, to transform the way people look at, experience, and care in the final chapter of life. For more information visit www.cypresshealing.com*

# Learning to Navigate

Bearing witness is not a passive act.
—Terry Tempest Williams

*Jonathan Bowman*

## What Is Home Care?

When hearing the term "home care" for the first time, it is not uncommon for caregivers to have feelings of confusion. The first exposure to the ambiguous and over-generalized terms of the home care industry prompts caregivers to seek answers from experts. This chapter focuses on answering the most common questions in a way that is easy to understand and can provide confidence in making choices for your loved one.

*When You Might Use Home Care*

Home care is a wide range of services that can be provided in your home or wherever you call home—such as an assisted living community, skilled nursing facility, etc.—from as little as one hour to a full twenty-four hours per day, and from once in a while to seven days a week. Home care services may include meal preparation, light housekeeping, laundry service, errand services, grocery shopping, medication management, and personal care. Activities of Daily Living (ADLs) are a big part of what home care professionals provide. ADLs, including showering, dressing, grooming, ambulating, and transferring, tend to be a big focus for seniors who hire home care professionals. Skilled nursing services can also be provided in the home. Physical, occupational, and speech therapies, IV infusions, wound care, social service, and educational activities are also a part of skilled nursing home care.

After a hospital stay, a fall, or a period in an acute rehab facility are the most common events that trigger caregivers to consult with a home care professional. These events are often preceded by the mismanagement of medication changes, cognitive deficiencies, episodes of severe memory loss or confusion, poor appetite, dehydration, severe and chronic pain, a fall, or the diagnosis of a terminal illness.

*Types of Home Health Care*

There are two primary types of healthcare services that can be provided in your home.

Skilled Home Health (aka Medicare Home Health)—Skilled services such as nursing (wound care, diabetic teaching, assessments, IV infusion, etc.), physical therapy, occupational therapy, and speech therapy can all be delivered at home and are typically covered by private insurance or Medicare. Skilled home care agencies require a written order (or prescription) from a physician to begin care. Medicare will pay for skilled home care if the patient is "homebound." Medicare will only continue to pay for the care if the providers document that the patient is making progress. Typically, this kind of assistance is authorized for only thirty days at a time. At the end of the thirty days, the patient's physician will reauthorize care if it is believed necessary and the patient still meets the "homebound" criteria.

Private Duty Home Care—This care does not require a physician's order and there is no criterion that must be met. The service is paid for privately (most of the time, but please read below about alternative payment options that might be available) and can start and stop whenever the care recipient and/or the family chooses. Private duty home care can be engaged anywhere from one hour to twenty-four hours per day. Services may include companion care (or "sitter" services), transportation to and from doctor's appointments, etc., meal preparation, light housekeeping, laundry service, errand services, grocery shopping, medication management, and personal care. Assistance with personal care and the activities of daily living tend to be a main focus of what home care professionals most often provide.

*Types of Providers*
For private duty home care, there are typically three types of service providers, each with specific benefits and drawbacks.

Home Care Agency—With a home healthcare agency, all the home care workers are direct employees of the company, which means that the agency pays all necessary payroll taxes, Workers Compensation insurance, and professional liability insurance. Additionally, the agency is responsible for training, ongoing scheduling (and back-up care if necessary), and case management for your loved one. In Florida all caregivers are required to go through a Level II federal fingerprint criminal history background check, and also must receive CPR training and Alzheimer's training in order to work for a home care agency.

The downside is that this agency model is the most expensive option, currently costing about $20 per hour on average; however, it provides significant protection for that fee.

There are actually two different types of home care agencies that provide services as well:

Companion Agencies are registered with the state to provide services but are not allowed to provide hands-on care to their clients. Typically these agencies focus on providing light housekeeping, meal preparation, transportation, and companionship.

Home Health Agencies are licensed by the state and highly regulated. (Some are also accredited by a national accreditation body, such as JACHO, CHAP, or ACHC.) A home health agency is able to provide all levels of care—from companionship to assistance with activities of daily living, to medication management. Typically, your loved one's care will be managed by a Registered Nurse on staff who will create the care plan and ensure it is adhered to.

Nurse Registry—This type of agency utilizes independent contractors as caregivers. The nurse registry screens candidates and clients and then makes a referral for each client and caregiver to work with each other. Because the caregiver is not an employee of the registry, the registry has very little say in their training, schedule, or duties while caring for the client. Those responsibilities typically fall to the clients and their families. Additionally, the client may be responsible for the caregiver's payroll taxes, and may be liable for any injuries that may occur, as the caregiver is not covered with the protection of Workers Compensation insurance.

The positive aspect of nurse registries is they often cost several dollars less per hour than agencies, and can provide multiple referrals of caregivers (they just can't manage them after the placement has been made). A typical nurse registry caregiver costs approximately $17 per hour.

Individual Person—Often times this is a neighbor down the street or someone you might know from church. Sometimes these people are picked out of an ad in the newspaper or online. Hiring an individual is often the most economical way to receive home care; however, it is also the most susceptible to issues. It is very important that you know and trust who you are hiring. Typically, the individual has not been adequately trained or screened (background check, skills, knowledge, etc.), so the unknown factor is very high. Unfortunately, some caregivers seek out offering this service specifically to take advantage of frail elders. Hiring an individual puts you and your family at the greatest risk for these issues. While this type of situation does often work, it is definitely the most risky.

Other factors to consider are that there is no back-up care available if the primary caregiver is not available, no nurse oversees the care plan, and there is no office to help mediate any issues that might arise.

The cost for an individual caregiver can vary greatly, ranging from a low of $10 an hour to as high as $20 hour.

Some Questions to Ask When Considering Home Care
- Are you an accredited agency?
- How long have you been in business?
- Are the caregivers direct employees (do they receive W-2s)?
- What is the hiring process you go through to employ your caregivers?
- Do you pay Workers Compensation insurance for your caregivers?
- Do you have back-up care available? What is your policy if my caregiver is sick or calls off at the last minute?
- Do you have live-in care available?
- What is your billing policy?
- Do I have to sign a contract?
- Do rates change on nights and weekends?

*When Is It Time to Start Considering Home Care?*
There are some very specific events that often prompt families to engage the help of a home care company. If you suspect that any of the following may be compromising your

loved one's ability to live independently at home, it is time to begin investigating home care options.

- Having a fall (the leading cause of injuries in adults over the age of sixty-five)
- Mismanagement of medications
- General weakness, unsteady gait, having difficulty walking
- Chronic pain that prohibits normal activities of daily living
- Poor nutrition (either not interested in food, or meals have mainly shifted to TV dinners)
- Lack of transportation to run errands, go to the doctor's office, get groceries, etc.
- Social isolation
- Compromised range of motion in any of the extremities
- Memory impairment
- An acute medical event (stroke, heart attack, surgery, etc.)
- Neglecting light housekeeping duties (such as doing the dishes, laundry, changing linens)
- Poor self-hygiene (not taking a shower regularly, unkempt hair and nails, etc.)

Speaking with your loved ones about the need for help at home to enhance their safety and quality of life is often a sensitive subject. To seniors, being told that they need home care can represent a loss of independence and can be a difficult discussion for them. When having "the talk" about needing assistance, often having a third party present can be helpful. Home care companies can send a representative to facilitate this conversation with you and your loves ones.

*Services Available*

Here are some of the services a home care professional can provide for your loved ones:

- Meal planning and preparation
- Grocery shopping
- Feeding assistance
- Medication reminders
- Light housekeeping, such as doing the dishes after a meal, changing linens, and doing laundry
- Companionship, such as playing cards, reading the paper
- Help with showering or bathing
- Help getting dressed or undressed
- "Tuck-in" service
- Continence care
- Assistance with ambulation
- Transportation to appointments

*Paying for Home Care*

There are various payment options when considering how to pay for home care:

Private Funds—Most of the time, home care services are paid for privately. Billing policies vary from company to company but, typically, home care companies bill bi-weekly and charge only for the amount of time that your loved one received care. Some companies require a two-week deposit in advance, some companies require electronic payment through credit card or electronic fund transfer, while others just send an invoice and payment is due upon receipt.

Long-Term Care Insurance—This can be a very effective way to help offset the cost of care. Policies vary greatly in what they cover, and it is important to understand the specifics of your policy. Typically, a long-term insurance company will require that you work with a home health agency, and that the company's nurse has performed a comprehensive assessment prior to starting care. Most policies require that, in order to be eligible for care, assistance must be needed with two or more activities of daily living (bathing, dressing, toileting, ambulation, feeding, continence care, etc.) or the person has significant memory impairment. Additionally, policies will differ in their elimination period (how long you must pay privately before the policy's coverage will begin), the maximum daily benefit (typically between $50 and $250 per day), and the lifetime policy benefit (which can be a capped dollar amount or a specific length of time).

Reverse Mortgage—This is a government-regulated program that allows you to leverage the equity in your home to receive money now, providing funds to pay for needed care and allowing you or the loved one to stay in the home.

VA—The Veterans Administration has two programs that may help pay for care. One is through the VA disability program and the other is the VA Aid and Attendance Benefit. Each can contribute a significant amount of money toward care of both the veteran and/or the surviving spouse. Contact your local Veterans Service Organization for more information.

Medicaid Waiver—There are some nursing home diversion programs available through Medicaid that can utilize funds to keep seniors at home instead of in a nursing home. Contact your local area agency on aging to find out about qualifying for this Medicaid benefit.

Medicare and Private Insurance—As previously discussed, unfortunately Medicare and private insurance do not pay for "non-medical" in-home care. Instead, they are available only to pay for skilled services for a short duration.

Please remember that when considering home care, it is important to start early. Don't wait until a crisis situation occurs to explore home care agencies and determine the right provider for you. By starting early, you can often prevent or delay placement into an assisted living facility. Additionally, just a little bit of care can go a very long way.

*Jonathan Bowman is founder and CEO of Harmony Home Health, a leading home healthcare agency serving caregiving families in the Tampa Bay area of Florida. For more information, visit www. harmonyhh.com*

*Mel Coppola*

# A Culture Change in the World of Aging

Recently someone said to me, "I've read some articles about nursing homes and assisted living communities that specialize in 'individualized' care. How do I find this type environment in my loved one's area?"

I was glad she was reading these articles. It tells me that, more and more, word is getting out that aging, and caring for others as they age, can be different from what it was in the past. What people are now reading about is part of a grass-roots movement called "culture change."

Culture change in this regard began in the early 1990s, with a group of passionate folks working in the long-term care arena. Their idea was to transform nursing homes into communities that honor and value both residents and those who work for and with them. They desired communities where the focus was on growth—not on the losses and declines normally associated with aging. Although these early pioneers sought change in all settings, the original focus was first on nursing homes because they were the most institutional in nature.

So let's start where they started. Most people cringe at the thought of ending up in a nursing home, and elderly family members often plead not to be put into one because of negative connotations associated with them.

Prior to the 19th century there was no age-specific housing for frail elderly to live out their days if they had no family. They were relegated to the almshouse—poorhouse, where they were housed among the insane, criminal, homeless, and inebriated. They were categorized as "needy" and a burden on society. In the late 1800s, some upscale society members began "homes" for some of society's upper crust—mostly women who, now with limited family and means, had once been pillars of society. But this was a very small percentage. Many older people still wound up in almshouses.

Fast-forward to the mid 20th century and the passage of Social Security, Medicare, and Medicaid benefits, and nursing homes began popping up to care for older adults in need. Of course the private sector became involved, and most became "warehouses" for the old and frail. By the 1970s, investigations found many of these institutions provided sub-standard care. Aging people feared having to end their days there and family members were torn with grief if they had no other choice. For the current cohort of elders we can now understand why they plead, "Please don't put me in a home." The horror stories are alive in their memories.

The nursing homes most of us now know look and feel like sterile hospital settings, with residents housed in small utilitarian rooms that allow them little or no privacy. The set-up is designed to make it easier for the staff to assist large numbers of residents quickly and efficiently. Generally, residents have little say over their day-to-day routines.

This brings us to the reason we need culture change for long-term care. What's needed is not new people. The people who work in these long-term care environments are some of the most caring people in the world. They come to this industry with giving, loving hearts. What is needed is a dramatic transformation of these institutional settings into communities where people want to live and work.

Although the culture change movement is just over twenty

years old, there is still a long way to go. Some key leaders have taken the bull by the horns and drastically transformed institutions into home-like settings, with empowered staff who are able to focus their attention on the individual, not just the task. But it will take your voice and the voice of many others demanding these changes to truly transform the way we care for our elders and people living with different abilities, wherever they call home.

*Key Concepts of Culture Change*

Language

One of the first things needed in order to transform long-term care is a shift in our thinking. Language plays a key role in this. Words become things and can change our perception.

Let's start with the word we use for our older population. Currently there is so much talk about what the "politically correct" term is. Older folks don't like "senior," and the word "elderly" denotes people who are frail and feeble. "Elder" is gaining popularity, as it denotes wisdom and knowledge and seems to have an air of respect and honor about it.

Another language change being embraced is "care partner," not only to replace caregiver but to include the elder, her- or himself, along with anyone else on the care partner team. Truly, that is what is needed: a team to come together to support an individual. In most situations, care partner teams already exist—they just are not called that. But using these words purposefully helps us change the perception that it is all on one person's shoulders. Care partners have told me that using this language actually helped them feel that a burden had been lifted from them.

There are many other language changes that need to be made by the people in the industry of elder care. Some of these are words that create what is called the "dependency factor"—words like diapers and bibs. In my world diapers and bibs are for babies, not for people who fought wars, raised children, ran corporations, and managed many lives. These are people who should be respected despite their need now for assistance with incontinence or eating. Let's bring dignity to them and call these items what they are—briefs and napkins.

By changing the words we use, we can start to change the world our elders live in. Let's create caring communities where people can grow and learn from each other, no matter what their positions or roles are in those communities.[1]

Relationships Are Key

How does the community go about getting to know your loved one? Is the focus only on your loved one's medical conditions? Those are very important, but not the core of who your loved one is. And if, in the admissions process, they do a good job of getting to know your loved one, how quickly and to whom is that information conveyed?

Almost without exception, unless the community embraces culture change, the daily tasks of personal care (including bathing, dressing, helping in the bathroom, oral care, etc.), as well as assistance with eating and medication assistance, take priority over anything else that occurs in the facility.

Most homes do not add to the minimum-mandated ratio of staff-to-residents, and the underpaid, minimum-wage staff member needs to complete, for example, the bathing of seven residents before breakfast. Not getting everyone taken care of could cost the aide her or his job. The time-constraint plus the

---

1. Many references here are made to communities such as assisted living facilities and skilled nursing facilities. However, culture change truly refers to organizations across the continuum of care, including private-duty home care, home healthcare, short term rehabilitation, and hospices, to name a few.

stress of needing the job doesn't bode well for time to chat with each elder, even if they were provided some personal information. Generally, there are staff rotations as well, which further inhibits the direct-care staff from getting to know the residents. Relationships are hard to form when a constant stream of new faces provides your care.

Organizations that embrace culture change understand that dedicated staff assignments are the key to happier care partnerships and deeper relationships. Who knows better how Mrs. Jones likes her shower than the person who assists her regularly?

Relationships, ones that build deeply over time, are the key to any good care experience.

Empowerment of Elders and Care Partners

In many care communities, the decisions as to when your loved ones bathe, when and what they eat, when they can use the bathroom (if they need assistance), and what "activities" they do during their days are generally made by management. It's simple economics. Their reason is so the least amount of staff can care for many people quickly.

But culture change proponents turn that upside down. They understand that not every resident likes to rise, get bathed (if it's their day), dressed, and be sitting at the dining room table by 8 a.m. I know it would not be my preference. Culture change communities work with their residents' preferred daily rhythms, so that someone who is used to showering or bathing in the evening can still do that without upsetting the apple cart.

Person-directed care is one of the chief values of the culture change movement. Elders should be in charge of their own lives as much as possible, in any setting in which they live. And the people closest to them, whether family members or direct-care staff, should be empowered to help that elder live in the most meaningful way. Which is on their terms, not on the terms of someone in upper management who doesn't really know the elder. This is a big difference!

Other Concepts

Generally speaking, more and more communities embracing person-directed care practices are also changing their dining methods and standards. Instead of having everyone at breakfast between 7 and 9 a.m. for example, residents are able to eat what they prefer when they prefer. Dining is not done for the convenience of the community but rather for the preferences of the elders who call the facility home.

Of course, in a home setting, elders should be able to choose the time of their meals according to their preferences, not according to the accessibility of people who assist them. Some communities are now offering twenty-four hour dining access, and the standard two or three choices for the lunch or dinner menu have been expanded to include foods based on their residents' favorites.

Meaningful engagement should be a part of everyone's life. Some communities have wonderful calendars filled with activities, but are they meaningful to your loved one? This is another culture change value: engagement in which elders wish to be involved, wherever they live.

Another is access to children, animals, and the outdoors. Why do we segregate one of our most precious commodities, our elders, away from another precious commodity, children? Culture change sees intergenerational groupings as a win-win! It's the same with pets and the availability of nature. Elders can continue to enjoy these if we made them more accessible.

Here is a list of Person-Centered Values and Principles, directly from the Pioneer Network website:

- Know each person
- Each person can and does make a difference
- Relationship is the fundamental building-block of a transformed culture
- Respond to spirit, as well as mind and body
- Risk-taking is a normal part of life
- Put person before task
- All elders are entitled to self-determination, wherever they live
- Community is the antidote to institutionalization
- Follow the Golden Rule: Do unto others as you would have them do unto you
- Promote the growth and development of all
- Shape and use the potential of the environment in all its aspects: physical, organizational, psychosocial/ spiritual
- Practice self-examination, searching for new creativity and opportunities for doing better
- Recognize that culture change and transformation are not destinations but a journey—always a work in progress.

*Determining If an Organization Is Using Culture Change Values*

Questions to Ask

If you are touring a community, you will, more than likely, be dealing with an admissions person or move-in coordinator. Most of your questions will be directed to them, but feel free to ask to speak to the administrator or executive director if the person you are dealing with doesn't have answers that satisfy you. Also, use your eyes, ears, and all your senses to balance the answers you receive with what your senses perceive.

Since you now know some of the principle values of culture change, you could ask straight out if the community is involved in culture change. More probing questions would be along the lines of:

- Do you offer your staff person-centered care training? If so, are direct-care workers included in that training along with leadership?
- How will you and your staff learn who my loved one really is and what makes her happy?
- Will my loved one have the same care staff on a regular basis?
- Will my loved one's preferred daily rhythm be honored in terms of sleeping, bathing, grooming, and eating?
- What types of choices are offered for meals? Will my loved one have input as far as favorite foods, snacks, and refreshments?
- What about the time for meals? My loved one often eats a late breakfast, a light snack in the mid afternoon, and enjoys dinner after 7 p.m. Will his schedule be accommodated?
- Will my loved one have open access to outdoor areas?
- Does your community have any pets, or are residents allowed to bring theirs?
- My loved one is sometimes up late. What type of engagement will there be after dinner?
- Will my loved one be permitted to make decisions as to how his or her day is structured?
- Will my loved one have a private room?
- I want to stay involved in my loved one's care. What

voice will I have once he or she moves in?

## What to Listen For, What to Look For

As mentioned earlier, sometimes the words you hear don't always add up to what you experience and see in the community. What things should you see? First and foremost, you should see happy people. Smiling staff and smiling residents are a sign that this is a good community. And they should not only smile at you when they are acknowledging you. After you have passed them, turn and see if those smiles are still there and are genuine.

People should also be engaged—not necessarily in an activity, but engaged with others. If there is an activity taking place while you are there, notice the type activity and the level of engagement of both staff and residents. What you don't want to see are residents lined up along the halls, sleeping in their chairs or wheelchairs just to be out of their rooms.

The community should be clean and uncluttered, with open areas for wheelchairs and walkers to pass through easily. It doesn't need to be modern or have current design trends, although it should be appealing to your loved one. You want to avoid the institutional look of long, unending hallways, and instead look for homey atmospheres. An older building or style, even with long hallways, can still be made to feel homey with some creativity.

The home/community should have a pleasant smell without seeming overly bleached and antiseptic, nor should there be an odor of urine.

Ideally, the community should have at least a couple of congregate areas (depending on how many residents it accommodates), such as living rooms, libraries, enclosed patios and porches, open patios and porches, etc., for residents to use when they wish to be out of their rooms or apartments. There should be options for groups, quiet conversations, reading, or spending some time alone. Look for these areas and note how residents are using them.

Are there places other than the dining room where residents can find a snack or refreshment without asking for help?

If at all possible, speak to some staff without their supervisors or any residents nearby. Ask if they like working there, and why. You want to hear comments such as they love working with people and/or elders, that it is a good community that really cares about them and the residents. If the staff who will care for your loved one feels cared about by management, they will pass that along to your loved one.

Also, try to talk to some residents, again, if possible, without staff nearby. Ask them how they like living there, and why. Ask if they would recommend it to their friends.

Many communities now offer respite care by the day or half-day. If you and your loved one seem to be leaning toward a particular community, why not try it out a time or two before making a firm decision? It could ease your loved one's transition considerably.


Most times your gut will tell you whether something is right for your loved one or not. I remember once when my aunt was in rehab, following a stroke that left her weakened. I visited one day and found her crying in the hallway, in a wheelchair and stinking of urine. This was "Mary Clean" who was not incontinent; she was just weak and needed someone to help her into the bathroom. But despite her requests no one came and she couldn't do it by herself. Now, in the hallway crying and asking for help, still no one stepped up to help her wash and change her clothes. She was ashamed of herself and humiliated. No one should have to feel that way! Thank goodness I arrived for an unannounced visit! You need to be sure to do the same.

The most important thing to remember is that you do have choices. Your voice, along with that of your loved one, is so important, not only for yourselves but for countless others.


Resources

The Eden Alternative—"The Eden Alternative® is an international, non-profit 501(c)3 organization dedicated to creating quality of life for Elders and their care partners, wherever they may live... Through education, consultation, and outreach, it currently offers three applications of its principles and practices to support the unique needs of various living environments, ranging from the nursing home to the neighborhood street." For more information, visit www.edenalt.org

Pioneer Network—"Pioneer Network was formed in 1997 by a small group of prominent professionals in long-term care to advocate for person-directed care. This group called for a radical change in the culture of aging so that when our grandparents, parents—and ultimately ourselves—go to a nursing home or other community-based setting it is to thrive, not to decline ... Pioneer Network is a center for all stakeholders in the field of aging and long-term care whose focus is on providing home and community for elders." For more information, visit www.pioneernetwork.net


*Mel Coppola is a passionate presenter, team builder, facilitator, educator and consultant in the field of aging care. Her areas of passion and expertise include person-directed care in all elder living environments. For more information visit www.heartsincare.com*

*Gary Joseph LeBlanc*

## Are You Part of the Sandwich Generation?

I am often offered the opportunity to hear, once again, the many voices of diverse caregivers. Their honest, heartfelt conversations concerning current trials and hardships are very moving.

I was surprised, however, when I realized that most of what these dear people were describing placed them smack dab in the middle of what is now known as the "Sandwich Generation." When I told them this, few had ever heard of the term, let alone knew it had anything to do with them and their situation.

In the early 1980s, the "Sandwich Generation" phrase was coined to describe the hard-working folks who, in the midst of raising their own children, suddenly found themselves also caring for their ailing parent or parents—thus the "sandwich" designation.

Originally this was thought to apply only to those who were in their fifties or sixties and in the thick of being caregivers, while still having an adult child or grandchild living with them.

Well, things have changed. Now, with the acceleration of cases of early onset dementia-related diseases being diagnosed, and the addition of other plaguing heath issues to the list, the "Sandwich Generation" is becoming more of a familiar household word.

One thing that is clear is that the sacrifices made by these families are endless. However, what I hear again and again is how unfair this is to the children still living at home. Well, I guess that depends upon one's perspective.

I agree that bringing a grandparent suffering from dementia into a home is not what one would expect to be a normal experience for a child or adolescent. But as the saying goes, "Things happen."

But here is a different angle: What a perfect opportunity to teach your kids some valuable lessons about life! Consider including them in decision making. Let them be an important cog in your family's wheel of care and communication. Allow them to observe for themselves that, indeed, yours is a strong and caring family, committed to each other no matter how dire the situation is. This can only be a good thing as it helps to build character. Hey, these are the kids that may likely be making decisions for you as you grow old!

I've never been one to believe in hiding things from children. I would say that most of them are very aware of their surroundings and are much more durable and resilient than we give them credit for. Being honest with them about what is transpiring will help prepare them for the inevitable, and it may assist in their understanding the behavioral changes they are witnessing.

Personally, I would include them in some of the caregiving duties that need to be performed. Many caregivers tell me how proud they are of their children for taking on the role of helping out with their loved ones.

We have to include the "Sandwich Generation" as being yet another phenomenon that has been partly caused by our present global financial situation. Today's "children" are staying in the comfort zone of their parents' nests much longer. Many venture out, only to quickly return because of financial difficulties. Include in this thought process the fact that there are many seniors today who simply cannot afford the high cost of a care facility.

I have to say that I don't see this "Sandwich Generation" fading away anytime soon. In fact, it may be with us for generations to come.

*Gary Joseph LeBlanc, a national speaker on dementia caregiving, is the author of* Staying Afloat in a Sea of Forgetfulness, The Aftereffects of Caregiving, Managing Alzheimer's and Dementia Behaviors, *and co-author of* While I Still Can. *His website is Common Sense Caregiving. For more information visit www.commonsensecaregiving.com*

## What is a Certified Geriatric Care Manager or Aging Life Care Specialist?

Navigating through the "healthcare maze" can be confusing, frustrating, even frightening. Having a private Geriatric Care Manager (GCM) can help lead you in the right direction and assist in making the best choices among providers in your community.

Since the field of private Geriatric Care Management is still relatively new, it is essential to educate the community about the services GCMs can provide, and the extensive training it takes to acquire the credential. The Case Management Society of America (CMSA) adopted a philosophy, in 2009, regarding case management. Stated in their standards of practice manual is that the underlying premise of case management is based in the fact that, when an individual reaches the optimal level of wellness and functional capability, everyone benefits. This includes the individuals being served, their support systems, the healthcare delivery systems, and the various reimbursement sources. Case Management serves as a means for achieving client wellness and autonomy thorough advocacy, communication, education, identification of service resources, and service facilitation in order to optimize the outcome for all concerned.

Geriatric Care Managers are experts who assist in many different areas, such as:

- Home care services—Assessing what types of services

are needed and assisting the family in monitoring those services.

- Medical management—Facilitating communication between doctor(s) and the family, attending doctor appointments, and monitoring the client's adherence to medical orders and instructions, if needed.
- Medication management—If the GCM is an RN, they can fill medication reminders and keep the doctor and family informed of possible side effects. They can suggest changing medication or even discontinuing certain meds when they are no longer needed.
- Communication—Keeping family members and other service providers informed as to the changing needs of the client.
- Legal—Consulting with elder law attorneys, providing an expert opinion for courts in determining the level of care of a client.
- Financial—Reviewing or overseeing bill payment or consulting with the client's accountants or Power of Attorney holder.
- Safety and security—Assessing and monitoring clients at their homes; making recommendations for a safe home; observing changes and potential risks of abuse or exploitation.
- Housing—Helping families evaluate and select the appropriate level of care needed for the client to stay at home, or residential options.
- Social—Suggesting and providing opportunities for the client to engage in social, recreational, or cultural activities that enrich the quality of their lives.

The GCM must have years of experience in the field of case management, as well as a degree in nursing, social work, psychology, gerontology, or other field related to aging and elder care, before they can sit for their credentialing exam. They must take up to eighty hours of continuing education each certification period. The main certifications one must possess to become a GCM are: CCM (Certified Case Manager), CMC (Case Manager Certified), C-ASWCM (Certified Advanced Social Work Case Manager, or C-SWCM (Certified Social Work Case Manager).

One way to find a GCM in your area is to through the ALCA, the Aging Life Care Association (formerly the National Association for Professional Geriatric Care Managers). In May of 2015, the ALCA rolled out a new name that is exclusive for Certified Care Managers. The certified individual is known as an Aging Life Care Manager or Specialist. Aging Life Care Managers are professionals who help facilitate services for our aging and disabled population. They often become the client's coach and guide when trying to find their way through the healthcare maze. This new name lets the general public know that the individual has gone through additional training in order to achieve certification. Geriatric Care Managers who are members of ALCA differ from elder- or patient-advocates, senior advisors or navigators, or even people who just call themselves Geriatric Care Mangers. ALCA members must meet the stringent education, experience, and certification requirements of the organization. All care managers are required to adhere to a strict code of ethics and standard of practice. They are required to prove their degrees and certifications, and have references. These GCMs have what you might call the "Betty Crocker Gold Seal of Approval"!

*Laura Freed, RN, BS, CCM, is the founder of Wishes 4 Wellness, LLC, Nursing Care Management, which focuses on medical management for disabled and older adults in Clearwater, Florida. For more information, visit www.Wishes4Wellness.com*

## Creating a Family Caregiver's Home Health Emergency Care Plan

Having been a caregiver for my mother and also helping with other family and friends, I know it is most important to have a written Home Health Emergency Care Plan. On occasion, family caregivers themselves become sick or may have an accident or require medical attention and help. As a caregiver advocate and support group facilitator, I see that most caregivers do not have an emergency plan.

I suggest you get yourself a notebook and write "Emergency Care Plan" on the front in bold, large letters. This notebook should have all the information someone would need to take over in your absence, if necessary.

What to include?

- Durable Power of Attorney for Health Care holder's name and all contact information.

- Family Contacts: List all the people who need to be called in case of an emergency, along with their telephone numbers and both physical and e-mail addresses.

- Medical Contact Information: Include names, addresses (physical and e-mail), and phone numbers (including cell phone and fax) of all the doctors who treat your care recipient. Be sure to include the dentist, eye doctor, ear doctor, etc.

- Insurance Information: List names, policy numbers, and where the policies are kept.

- Medications: First note where you keep the medications. Second, list the name of each drug, its dosage, and how frequently each should be dispensed to your loved one. Third, add any medications they may be allergic to. For each medication, note the doctor who prescribed it and list the pharmacy and hospital names and addresses.

- Testing Needs: If your loved one requires high blood pressure or diabetes testing, list the frequency and optimal target ranges. Include the names and phone numbers of the doctors' offices to contact.

- Meals and Food: First, list all foods that are not allowed, due to allergies or drug interaction. List the times of day your loved one eats and some examples of menus they enjoy. Be sure to note if your loved one (especially in dementia cases) prefers to eat from a certain bowl or dish.

- Daily Routine: Provide detailed instructions for toileting requirements, transfers, showers, dressing, etc. If your loved goes for a walk or naps at the same time each day, or watches a certain television program, please note it. Some dementia patients prefer to watch television without the sound. Also, some dementia patients respond to or are calmed by certain music. If so, please note this.

- Home Health Care Services: Your emergency plan should include the contact information for a professional home care company that you have researched and with which you feel comfortable in case there is no one to step in for you.

Additionally, if you have a pet, it would be wise to include information regarding its care and feeding, including the name and phone number of someone who could look after the pet, boarding options if necessary, and the veterinarian's information.

If you are a caregiver without a Home Health Emergency Care Plan, begin one today. Even if you don't think anything is ever going to happen, you will have the peace of mind of knowing you're prepared. Then be sure to let others know where to find the care plan if they ever need to!

*Linda Burhans is a caregiver advocate and author of the book* Good Night and God Bless: Celebrating Love, Laughter & the Lessons of Loss. *For more information, visit www.LindasCaregiverConnections. com*

*Stephanie M. Edwards*

## Are You Legally Prepared for Incapacity?

You are sitting in a crowded waiting room and there is a television playing a show that is not one of your favorites. You wish you could lower the volume or turn the television off or, better yet, change the channel to a more enjoyable show.

You can't, however, because it isn't your television and you don't have the remote control. So, you just hope that your name is called quickly and you don't have to listen to the annoying television program for very long.

This is the predicament people find themselves in when they do not have incapacity planning documents in place. By doing nothing, they have handed the remote control to the state and have agreed to watch the television show the state chooses for them. This show is called "The Default Plan."

How do you keep possession of your remote control instead of handing it over? You maintain possession by putting your legal incapacity documents in place.

Is there a deadline for putting these incapacity documents in place? Absolutely.

If you wait too long and you become incapacitated before your documents are in place, then you forfeit your remote control and become subject to your state's default plan.

What incapacity planning documents should you put in place? In general, the documents consist of:

1.  Designation of Health Care Surrogate

2.  Living Will
3.  Durable Power of Attorney.

Collectively, these are called your advance directives.


*What Is the "Designation of Health Care Surrogate"?*

The Designation of Health Care Surrogate states who you have chosen to make medical decisions for you and communicate those medical decisions if you become no longer able do so yourself.

Being the health care surrogate is a challenging job because the surrogate has to follow your wishes and not their own during emotionally volatile situations. It is best to designate only one person to serve as your surrogate, and name one or more alternate surrogates to serve one after the other, not simultaneously, if the previously named surrogate is not able to act on your behalf.

What is the state default plan if you don't put a Designation of Health Care Surrogate in place? I cannot speak to each individual state, but the practice in Florida can provide a general outline of understanding. It is important you learn what laws are in place in the state where you or your loved one reside.

In Florida, a health care proxy will be appointed to act in the event you become incapacitated and cannot make decisions for yourself. The person appointed as your health care proxy is chosen in the order spelled out under State law. For most people, the spouse is named as the health care proxy. If you do not have a spouse, then it will be your adult children, followed by your parents (if living), and then your adult siblings.

At first glance the default plan may look like the selection you would make yourself. The default plan's potential downfall is that as soon as you move past the spouse, there may be more than one person with equal authority to make decisions for you. If all the people with equal authority don't agree (because, of course, your children never disagree with each other) then decisions about your medical care could end up being made by a judge in a court proceeding.

This is obviously not the result that most people want for themselves or their families.


*What Is a Living Will?*

A Living Will's sole purpose is to state whether you do or do not wish to be kept alive artificially. Putting a Living Will in place is one of the most thoughtful favors you can do for your family and your health care surrogate. By clearly stating your wishes you can avoid devastating family disagreements and give your health care surrogate peace of mind that he or she is indeed making the decision you would have made yourself.

It is important to understand that a Living Will is different from a Do Not Resuscitate Order (DNR).

- A DNR specifically addresses whether you will or will not receive life saving medical procedures, such as CPR.

- A DNR is a doctor's order that is available only from a doctor.

- The DNR, not the Living Will, is what emergency medical personnel responding to a call to your home will need to see in order to refrain from giving you or your loved one medical procedures, such as CPR.

What is the default plan if you don't have a Living Will in place? Your health care surrogate or proxy will make the decision. If there is any disagreement about what your end-of-life wishes are, then once again a court proceeding will be required before the decision is made to remove or keep in place medical devices keeping you alive artificially.

*What is the Durable Power of Attorney?*

The person you name to act on your behalf under the Durable Power of Attorney makes all the non-medical, day-to-day operational decisions for you (except if you have a trust; then the financial decisions are split between the agent under the Durable Power of Attorney and the successor trustee under your trust).

The agent's job is very broad and in general involves determining how to best take care of you and your assets. You give your agent a great deal of power, so it is vitally important that you choose someone you trust for this job. You can choose to name one primary agent and then one or more alternate agents who can step in one after the other, if for any reason your primary agent cannot act on your behalf.

You may decide that you want to name two primary agents to act together. Depending upon whom you choose, this may be a way for two agents to successfully share the extensive duties that have to be performed by an agent, or it can be a fast track to a court proceeding if the two agents cannot agree.

What is the default plan if you don't put a Durable Power of Attorney in place? The default option is a guardianship proceeding in court, where a judge will appoint a guardian for you. This guardian may or may not be a family member or the person you would have chosen yourself. The judge will make the decision that he or she feels is in your best interest, but has no way to know your preference.


*What Is Legal Capacity and Does Your Loved One Still Have It?*

The question of whether your loved one still has the legal capacity to sign advance directives is not an easy one to answer. In general, your loved one has to be able to understand the nature of the document being signed and the decisions and powers being delegated.

Sometimes a determination of legal capacity requires collaboration between an elder law attorney, your loved one's doctor, and a geriatric care manager.

Of course, whenever possible, the best way to avoid legal capacity becoming a debatable question is to seize control of the remote control and put your advance directives in place before illness or injury strikes.


*Who Should You Choose to Speak for You in Your Advance Directives?*

Choosing whom to appoint to speak for you can be an overwhelming and emotional decision. If you are married, your spouse may seem to be the natural choice. Some spouses, however, don't want to be the one to make end-of-life decisions, and some spouses are unavailable to act due to illness or injury.

If you don't have a spouse, then choosing your oldest child may feel like the way to avoid hurting anyone's feelings and preserving family harmony. Oldest children have many talents, but being the oldest doesn't automatically mean he or she has the temperament, experience, or time to be a health care surrogate or an agent under a Durable Power of Attorney. Every child isn't suited for every job. Try to match the child you choose to the requirements of the job.

For the health care surrogate, you need a person who can be a vocal advocate for your medical care and who is strong enough to remember your wishes, rather than their own, when difficult decisions have to be made. For the agent under your Durable Power of Attorney, you need the person who can be absolutely trusted to do the right thing with your money.

Once you make your choices you can enhance the chances

that the surrogate and the agent act as you would like by talking with them. Share your philosophy about how you define quality of life and what you consider to be good financial decisions on your behalf.

Being a surrogate or an agent is a hard job. Don't make it harder by avoiding talking with your surrogate and agent because you (or they) don't want to think about your becoming incapacitated. If you don't have the conversation, you risk saddling them with lifelong, haunting doubts about whether they acted in accordance with your wishes.


*How Do You Bring Up the Topic of Advance Directives?*

How do you bring up the subject of incapacity and encourage your loved ones to put these advance directives in place before a crisis strikes?

Let's be honest. Incapacity is not likely to be the preferred topic of conversation while everyone is together at the Thanksgiving dinner table. Incapacity can be an uncomfortable subject. If a prognosis of likely incapacity is not already in the picture for the family, then very few people want to acknowledge that they may become incapacitated in the future. If a prognosis of likely incapacity is already in the picture, then many times the family is uncomfortable with the subject because no one feels they know the correct thing to say.

Sometimes you can casually bring up the subject of incapacity as a comment related to a story in the news or to a situation that is affecting an acquaintance of the family. Perhaps you can turn the next actual tussle for the television remote control into the opening you need. No matter how much resistance you receive to your attempts to start the conversation, keep trying. Nothing can disrupt family harmony faster, in the emotional situations that incapacity creates, than different family members believing wholeheartedly in different versions of what they think you want.

*Why Should You Put Advance Directives in Place Today?*
Because tomorrow always comes too soon.

*Stephanie M. Edwards founded Edwards Elder Law, P.A. in St. Petersburg, Florida, which focuses exclusively on the needs of seniors, veterans, and their families. She provides legal services that address immediate care concerns, proactive plans for the future, and coping during times of crisis. For more information, visit www. edwardselderlaw.com*

## How Do You Keep Your Financial Plan on an Even Keel?

Financial planning should ideally be started while you're young, and then reviewed and revised regularly as the years roll by and your needs evolve. Life, however, is sometimes not ideal and the best-laid plans can go astray. How do you keep your well-intended plans on an even keel, knowing that the winds of life can force a change in direction?

Take a moment and think about your financial plan as a well-designed sailboat. The hull is the right length to support the mast and the sails. The boat rests on a keel, which is the right depth and weight for the boat. There is a wheel in the cockpit to steer by and a compass to keep the boat on course. There is a life preserver hanging off of the stern railing and a life jacket for each passenger on board. If you are an experienced sailor, you might choose to sail this boat yourself, or you could have a captain and crew on board so that you can sit back, relax, and watch the clouds float by. This is your sailboat, so you can imagine it in any way that works for you.

For a moment, think about the hull of your well-designed sailboat as your Cash Management Plan. Envisage the sails as your Asset Management Plan, the life preserver hanging on the stern, and the life jackets on board as your Risk Management Plan. If all is designed the way it should be and the weather is fair, your financial life should flow smoothly and produce the results that will help make your life the way you dreamed it could be.

Cash Management is the part of your financial plan which concerns the cash you have in a bank account, in CDs, or hidden under your mattress. Cash Management is like the hull of the sailboat. It provides the base on which your financial plan rests. Without proper cash management, there would be no financial plan because there would be no money to fund the plan.

Asset Management is the part of your financial plan that concerns your investments. These are your stocks, bonds, mutual funds, and your fixed assets, such as your home, your car, and your sailboat.

Risk Management is the part of your financial plan that concerns the protection of your cash, your assets, and yourself. Simply stated, risk management is your insurance.

If a sailboat is designed with an overly heavy keel and a hull that is too long for the height of the mast or the number and size of the sails, the boat will be under-powered and will only move sluggishly as the sails struggle to capture enough wind to move the boat forward. If the wind dies, your poorly designed boat will wallow in the swells. If the captain wants to turn the boat to take advantage of a shift in the wind, it will take a long time to make that change of direction.

Like this heavy and underpowered sailboat, if your financial plan concentrates too much on cash, you will have a hard time producing the kind of results needed to move your financial life forward. In a low interest-rate environment like the one we have experienced over the recent past, your money is not able to work for you. This "lazy money" usually doesn't decrease in value, but it doesn't increase much either. It may make you feel "safe," but in fact, too much cash causes you to wallow in the swells. It is important to have some cash on hand for day-today necessities and emergency funds, but keeping all or most of your financial resources in cash is counterproductive to a healthy financial future.

If your sailboat has a good, strong hull and keel you will need a set of sails to power the boat. Most sailboats have several different sets of sails, which can be changed according to weather conditions. A boat with well-trimmed sails moves swiftly through the water and can be turned as the direction of the wind changes or when you decide to go in a different direction. When a storm arises, sails can be adjusted so that the boat is not over-powered. A good captain knows when and how to adjust the sails for maximum performance and to avoid having the sails torn to bits by the wind.

The Asset Management part of your financial plan is analogous to the sails on your boat. Just as too much sail can put your boat in danger, too much risk in your asset portfolio can put your financial future in jeopardy. If the wrong type of sail is set for the weather at hand, the boat can flounder or the sail can be shredded by the winds. If all of your investments are in high-risk, high-flying stocks, the thrill of the ride might be great until something changes, and all of a sudden you could find yourself riding the downside of a monster wave. Many people love to race sailboats or get a thrill from putting up the maximum amount of sail possible, heeling the boat way over on its side, straining the hull and rigging. Some people get a thrill from taking a bet on a high-flying stock or market sector. This is fine, as long as you don't mind risking the loss of your sailboat or the loss of your money, which may or may not be recoverable.

If all your assets are in fixed assets, such as real estate, remember that one day it may be necessary to sell the asset to create cash for an emergency. As has been shown over the recent past, real estate can take a dive as deep as a sailboat plunging into the trough between high waves. If you find yourself in the trough at the same time life hands you a challenge that requires cash, you could find yourself in serious trouble.

Your Risk Management should be just as carefully thought out as your Cash and Asset Management. Too much insurance makes no more sense than having too little insurance. It's true that when the weather gets rough on the high seas, it's time to put on your life jacket and make sure that the life preserver on the stern is ready for possible action. Not only should your boat—and your other fixed assets—be covered by insurance, your life, your health, and your possible long-term care should all be covered in case the need arises.

Stop a moment and imagine your well-trimmed sailboat with a huge life preserver hanging off the stern. This life preserver is so large and so heavy that the entire boat is off balance, with its bow way higher in the water than the stern. And, what about those personal life jackets on board? If you sail with a maximum of six passengers, why would you need twenty-five life jackets?

Insurance is the aspect of your financial plan intended to help you feel "safe." Life insurance will help a loved one in the case of your demise. Disability insurance will provide income for you and your family if you should become disabled and can no longer work. Health insurance is an obvious necessity in today's reality. Long-term care insurance will provide peace of mind to your family, in knowing that your entire financial plan will not be devastated by the costs of long-term care. Each of these types of insurance should be considered at different life stages. Just as it would be foolish not to have automobile insurance or homeowners insurance, it would be foolish to ignore the security offered by life, health, disability, and long-term care insurance.

If you take your sailboat out in a storm and get into trouble, your life jackets and life preserver must already be on board and ready to use. There is no way that you can magically produce life preservers for your passengers if you did not put them on board before the sailboat left the port in sunny weather. It is exactly the same with insurance. With the exception of health insurance, which is now available without regard to pre-existing conditions, you must obtain insurance before the need arises. If you have a terminal condition, you cannot get life insurance. If you have had an accident and are disabled, you cannot get disability insurance. If you are already in need of long-term care, you cannot obtain long-term care insurance. Above all, you must be in generally good health to be insurable.

Any insurance and the costs associated with it must be carefully considered as a part of your overall financial plan and not as a stand-alone purchase sitting somewhere outside of that plan. Being over-insured is often a result of purchasing insurance that is not treated as a part of your overall plan and which may not be appropriate for your age or your life stage.

Fixed annuities are considered to be insurance products, while variable annuities are generally considered to be investment products. The range and scope of possible annuity choices is enormous and these are often very complicated financial instruments. It is definitely desirable to discuss any annuity purchase with your financial planning professional, to make sure the annuity being proposed is right for you and your financial well-being.

There is a single phrase that is often used as a nautical blessing: "Fair winds and following seas." This is a wish for the sailor that the wind does not blow too hard, and that the sea is not too rough and helps propel the sailboat forward. In the financial planning world, the wish should be much the same. With an experienced financial planner to help, and a plan which is a living document designed to change over time and as protection needs increase, your financial well being should be like a well trimmed sailboat.

Enjoy!

*Candy Goodwin, CLTC, has been associated with Vernick Financial Planning in Seminole, Florida, since 2010. She concentrates on risk management and has extensive experience in long term care insurance. Candy also has several years experience working in the long-term care profession. For more information visit www.vernickfinancial.com*

Securities offered through:
Cadaret Grant and Co, Inc. Member FINRA/SIPC
Cadaret Grant and Co., Inc. and Vernick Financial Planning are separate entities

## What Is a Reverse Mortgage and How Does It Work?

Let's start with the basics. The federally insured Home Equity Conversion Mortgage (HECM) was instituted in 1989. The Federal Housing Authority (FHA) wanted to give senior homeowners a way to receive additional income by giving them access to the equity in their homes without taking on the burden of having to make monthly payments, such as are required by accessing a home equity line of credit. To make sure the needs of seniors were addressed, they looked to AARP for input as they designed the program. The result is one of the safest and most flexible finance options available for seniors today.

The FHA reverse mortgage is federally insured and guaranteed. It allows seniors over the age of sixty-two to borrow against the equity in their homes without making monthly payments in return or having to sell the home. Funds from a reverse mortgage are considered loan proceeds and are not taxable.

The money can be used for any purpose that you wish. Often our clients use the available funds to pay off an existing mortgage, freeing up that monthly payment for other uses. Many also use the available funds to supplement their Social Security and pension incomes, for medical expenses, travel, home repairs, and ever-increasing property taxes or insurance bills. We also have seen many clients use the reverse mortgage as an emergency line of credit they can access in times of uncertainty or financial hardship.

The FHA-insured reverse mortgage (or HECM, as FHA calls it) is probably the most misunderstood financial product of modern times. Many people over-complicate the concept, leading to confusion and mistrust. With a reverse mortgage there is no transfer of ownership, any more than there is with a traditional mortgage, which is called a forward mortgage. Title to the home and equity always remain with the homeowner. The lender does not take the house. When you get a reverse mortgage, you never give up title or ownership in your home.

A reverse mortgage is the same as any other mortgage or home equity line of credit in almost every other way. Ask a question about a reverse mortgage and the answer is probably the same as with a forward mortgage. You borrow money, and receive a statement in the mail (either monthly or quarterly, depending on the company). The statement tells you how much you owe and how much interest was charged during the previous period, just like the statement you would receive with a traditional mortgage that you are paying down.

The first big difference with the reverse mortgage is that when that statement arrives you have no obligation to pay anything. You can make a payment if you want, but most borrowers don't. This contrasts with a traditional mortgage, where you typically would pay the interest charged and possibly some of the principal. Since you didn't make a payment on the reverse mortgage, when your statements arrive they will show that you owe a little bit more. The interest charged over the period since the last statement is added to your outstanding balance.

You continue in this manner as long as you or your spouse live in the home. This might be for a few years, until you decide to move, or may be several decades until you both pass away, at which time your heirs typically would sell the home. Whenever the time comes—through a decision to move or death, that you no longer live in your home, you or your heirs would sell the home and pay off the balance of the reverse mortgage and accrued interest. Just as with a traditional mortgage, whatever money is left after paying off the reverse mortgage balance still belongs to you or your estate.

The program intends that you will always have equity in your home. It is anticipated that as your interest accumulates and your loan balance increases, your home's value will increase enough to offset the accumulating debt, so there should be equity for you or the estate throughout the life of the loan.

### A Typical Scenario

Let's look at an example of a homeowner with a $300,000 house taking out a reverse mortgage, say, to pay off an existing mortgage in the amount of $180,000. After ten years, if the house were to appreciate at four percent per year the home value would now be $444,073, while their loan balance would have increased to approximately $321,300. This assumes they take a slightly higher interest rate as a trade-off for paying virtually no closing costs

### Is There a Down Side?

What if the real estate market crashes again? As we saw in 2008 through 2010, increases in home values are not guaranteed. In fact, borrowers who took out reverse mortgages from about 2005 through 2008 and whose loans have come due since then (because they decided to move or died) in most cases were not able to sell their homes for enough to pay off their reverse mortgage balance. With a traditional forward mortgage they would have been in the same negative equity position and personally liable for repayment of the shortfall.

But, a reverse mortgage borrower in the same situation has no personal liability for themselves or their estate. With an FHA-insured reverse mortgage there is no liability beyond the value of the property. While you or your heirs would not come away from the closing with any money, there also is no obligation to pay the shortfall on the debt because the FHA pays it. This is the second big difference between a reverse mortgage and a traditional mortgage.

An FHA-insured reverse mortgage is a "non-recourse" loan. In other words, when the time comes to sell the home, should the balance owed exceed the value of the house there is no personal liability or responsibility to the borrower or the estate. FHA steps in and pays the difference. Under normal economic conditions this FHA guarantee should not be a factor.

One of the most common issues or complaints about reverse mortgages is that someone who took out a reverse mortgage before the real estate market crash is now buried in their home debt. If you analyze this you will see that those people actually made out very well by taking out a reverse mortgage.

Let's look at another example of a $300,000 house where the borrower took out a reverse mortgage in 2005 for $180,000. Let's assume the borrower passed away in 2015. Their reverse mortgage balance may have increased to $321,300 while the home value dropped below $300,000. As you can see, this borrower was able to borrow more money in 2005 than the house may be worth in 2015 with no obligation to repay. That's a great outcome for the borrower.

The FHA has done a good job of adjusting available proceeds and their fees to ensure the long-term viability of the HECM program, so it will not become a burden on the American taxpayer down the road.

*Uses of a Reverse Mortgage*

The complexion of the reverse mortgage industry has changed dramatically over the years. The FHA-insured reverse mortgage is no longer considered a rescue device. The typical borrowers today are in their early sixties, and have excellent credit and upper-level income. About half of our clients have a free and clear home and utilize the increasingly popular reverse mortgage line of credit. The built-in credit line growth rate feature means that the unused portion of the line of credit will grow each year. The other half of our clients are using the reverse mortgage to pay off an existing mortgage and free up their monthly mortgage payment for other uses.

We have closed reverse mortgage loans for some of Florida's wealthiest families. Wealthy clients are being advised by their financial planners to look into reverse mortgages as part of their retirement financial planning. The strategy these financial planners suggest is to establish a reverse mortgage line of credit to draw on, rather than pulling money from retirement savings in the current economy.

One borrower we worked with had very little equity, so he brought $60,000 to closing in order to pay off an existing mortgage. By doing so, this borrower makes no monthly principal or interest payments for as long as he lives in the home as his primary residence. As always, he will have to continue to pay his property taxes, homeowners insurance, and HOA fees and maintain the property to FHA standards. This is becoming more and more common. One couple in another community recently brought $110,000 to the closing table, which, along with the proceeds from their reverse mortgage, paid off a substantial existing mortgage. They said, "Even laying out $110,000, we will break even on cash flow in less than five years, and look forward to another twenty or more years after that with no monthly mortgage payment!" Another client we met with owns a \$1.5 million home in Palm Beach. He has no existing mortgage and is looking to tap into some of his home's equity without the burden of monthly mortgage payments. This particular customer has the option of using either an FHA-insured reverse mortgage or a jumbo reverse mortgage program that is available.

The uses of reverse mortgages are endless. From paying off a home equity line of credit that's coming due, to closing a loan in eight days to stop a foreclosure, to funding a divorce settlement, the FHA Home Equity Conversion Mortgage is a great financial planning tool to fund the baby boomer retirement.

*Interest Rates*

Both fixed-rate and adjustable-rate reverse mortgages are available. Reverse mortgages traditionally have been adjustable rate mortgages. An adjustable-rate reverse mortgage is not nearly as onerous as a traditional adjustable-rate mortgage. The issue with the traditional adjustable-rate mortgage is that, if interest rates go up, the payment can become unaffordable to the borrower and result in foreclosure. This cannot happen with a reverse mortgage, since there is no requirement to make a payment.

As rates go up and rates come down it is simply a matter of interest to see what is being charged on the statement each month. The important thing to focus on with a reverse mortgage, in deciding between an adjustable rate and a fixed rate, is what are rates likely to average over your lifetime, as individual peaks and valleys have little effect on the day-to-day life of the reverse mortgage borrower.

In addition to interest, the borrower is charged an FHA fee, which currently is 1.25 percent of the outstanding loan balance per year.

*Where Does the Money Come from?*

No matter where you get a reverse mortgage, the process is the same. Your loan will be processed and underwritten, followed by a closing and funding. Usually within thirty days after closing, the reverse mortgage will be insured by FHA and then sold, through Ginnie Mae, to a large institutional investor on the secondary market, such as an insurance company, sovereign fund, or pension fund.

These loans are sold in large packages of $6 million or more. The sale of these loans doesn't affect you, the borrower, as the borrower's sole point of contact is with the servicing company. With FHA guaranteeing the end-value of the home, these large investors are willing to accept a very low interest rate. The result is an attractive package for many borrowers.

*Who Sells Reverse Mortgages?*

The reverse mortgage industry is made up of a few large national companies that write tremendous volume but spend huge amounts of money on advertising. You've probably seen their commercials on cable television networks. These companies are typically structured as a call center. The borrower is cast into a high-volume situation with "the next available operator" kind of scenario.

At the other end of the spectrum are forward or traditional mortgage companies that claim to do reverse mortgages. The average forward mortgage broker does fewer than two reverse mortgages per year, resulting in a lack of expertise that creates a lot of problems for the credibility of the reverse mortgage industry.

Between the extremes of the large national companies and the part-time forward mortgage brokers, there are regional companies that do reverse mortgages exclusively. They are in a position to write enough loans to be truly expert while delivering lower costs and a higher level of customer service. While many of these companies are technically brokers, the fact is that no matter where you get your loan, from either a lender or broker, it's going to end up being sold through Ginnie Mae. So, practically speaking, everyone in the reverse mortgage business is really a broker, in that they are not, ultimately, lending their own money.

There are many good companies but there are also a lot of high-pressure, less scrupulous people, as you will find in any industry. As with any major purchase, the importance of research cannot be overemphasized. Your local or state Better Business Bureau is a good place to start, along with the National Reverse Mortgage Lenders Association website, and the National Mortgage Licensing System website, which allows you to review the employment record of any individual mortgage broker you are dealing with.

*Who and What Qualifies?*

FHA rules require that at least one borrower on the reverse mortgage be sixty-two or older. With some limitations, it is possible to do a reverse mortgage with one spouse under the age of sixty-two, who will still enjoy contractual rights to stay in the house for life.

While there is no set minimum credit score, borrowers must demonstrate an ability and willingness to pay their ongoing obligations, including housing costs, other debts and commitments, and an allowance for basic living expenses.

Many property types qualify, ranging from manufactured homes (with some limitations) to multi-million dollar beach-front mansions and almost everything in between. (High-value homes are, however, limited on the amount that can be borrowed.) Condos are eligible but require a special FHA approval by the entire association, and only principal residences qualify. Yet FHA rules even allow multi-family residences, up to a four-plex. However, most, if not all, lenders are reluctant to lend on anything more than a duplex. Even so, a duplex with a reverse mortgage presents a very attractive positive cash flow opportunity if handled properly.

*What Is the Future of the Reverse Mortgage?*

In the early 1960s my father was a regional manager for Household Finance Corporation. You may remember HFC as the place people went if they needed a small loan. HFC offices usually were upstairs from or in the back of a store, never right out in the open, on the theory that people were ashamed to be seen borrowing money.

My father was passed over for a promotion that he thought he deserved. His boss assumed that, because my father had ten children to support, he would never resign. He did. He left HFC and went to work for a small startup company, which, under his leadership, grew to be a major competitor of HFC and ultimately was bought out by a large conglomerate, Avco Finance. Under my dad's leadership, Avco became the largest consumer loan company in the world. The key to Avco's success was that they put their offices in storefronts out in the open for all to see.

Where are HFC and Avco today? That industry is pretty much gone now due to the common use of credit cards. Today, when you stand in the checkout line at the grocery store and the person ahead of you pays with a Visa card, is your first thought that they may be experiencing some financial difficulty? Of course not, yet what they are doing isn't really any different than having gone to HFC fifty years ago. Credit cards are just a way of life now. I believe the reverse mortgage is in the "HFC stage" today, and five years from now a reverse mortgage will be regarded as the wise and necessary mainstream financial tool that everyone will consider as an option in developing a responsible financial plan for retirement.

It is simple arithmetic that for us baby boomers to maintain our standards of living, there will have to be more funding coming from somewhere. Most baby boomer equity is tied up in our homes. I see it like this: You have a 401k or IRA you can draw money from, and you have home equity from which you can draw additional funds in much the same way. Both are assets that can be left to your heirs. Both can go up or down in value. Why not consider taking advantage of both options?

Every borrower has a unique situation that deserves a thorough evaluation and consultation. With this information I hope you have a better understanding of how a reverse mortgage might benefit your financial situation.

*Malcolm Tennant is a co-founder of Access Reverse Mortgage Corp. Access was founded in Florida over eleven years ago and is recommended by many professionals and organizations including National Aging in Place Council, Better Business Bureau and National Reverse Mortgage Lenders Association. Malcolm is a leading expert on reverse mortgages and one of only twelve Certified Reverse Mortgage Professionals in Florida. He regularly appears as an expert contributor on various radio shows. For more information, visit www.accessreversemortgage.com*

*Karyn Rizzo*

## How Can I Access Veteran Benefits?

*It takes the courage and strength of a warrior to ask for help.*
*—Author Unknown*

Our veterans, regardless of age, many times are not aware of benefits they may be entitled to because of their service.

It has been astonishing for me to learn that the men and women who have sacrificed their lives and safety for us are not always aware they have access to free or low-cost healthcare at any local VA hospital, depending on their service connection status and income criteria. Many are never "debriefed," if you will, when they leave the military, and some do not know benefits they are entitled to for life.

Some seniors with access to free or low-cost healthcare at a local VA hospital never utilize it, either because they don't know they have the benefit or because they think they will receive substandard healthcare.

Most VA hospitals are staffed with excellent medical professionals and are equipped with the latest in medical testing, equipment, and programs. However, some regions have better programs than others. Some VA hospitals offer a variety of specialty programs that are unique and impressive.

Aside from having a primary care physician, veterans also receive free or low-cost co-payments on any testing and medications they may need. They also can receive assistance for mental health issues, such as post-traumatic stress disorder (PTSD). For some veterans and their families, this is an extreme help to them financially.

The additional medical services veterans are eligible for include nursing, therapy, and social services in the home, plus oxygen and medical equipment. The services are either free or have low co-payments, depending on the veteran's service connection status and/or income criteria.

There are two requirements to access the VA healthcare system. The veteran must have received an honorable discharge, and will need his or her DD 214. Getting started begins with enrollment. Veterans can now apply and submit the VA Form 1010EZ application for enrollment on-line. Veterans can also enroll by calling 1-877-222-VETS (8387) Monday through Friday from 8 a.m. to 8 p.m. (Eastern), or by visiting at any VA healthcare system or VA regional benefits office. Once enrolled, they can receive health care at any VA health care facility nationwide.

Each VA hospital system has a care management team to coordinate patient care and ensure that veterans receive patient-centered, specific access to the care and benefits they're entitled to.

While many veterans may qualify for free healthcare services, most need to submit an annual financial assessment to determine if they qualify. Veterans with income that exceeds the established limits and those who choose not to submit a financial assessment are charged nominal co-payment fees for physicians' visits and medications provided through the VA.

Certain services are not charged a co-payment at all. These apply to publicly announced VA health fairs and outpatient visits dedicated to preventative screening, such as vaccinations for influenza (flu), or specific diagnostic screenings, such as hypertension, hepatitis C, tobacco, alcohol, certain cancers, and HIV.

For some, a VA healthcare system may not be close by or easy to access. There is, however, reimbursement for travel costs that some veterans and/or their support system may be eligible for. In some cases, the VA will provide the needed transport, such as a wheelchair van, or an ambulance when necessary. Eligibility for transport or travel-cost reimbursement can be determined by and coordinated through the care management team.

Veterans and their families wanting access to a wide range of information and services can also visit Make the Connection: Videos & Info for Military Veterans for more helpful information.

*Mental Health Care Treatment*

We've seen a growing number of aging veterans who may be struggling without knowing they are entitled to these programs, as well as help for their support system to manage behaviors and health care needs at home.

Veterans who need access to trained mental health professionals should call the Veteran Crisis Lifeline at 1-800-273-TALK (8255). This hot-line is available twenty-four hours a day, seven days a week. More information about VA Mental Health Benefits is available on the Internet.

*Aid and Attendance Benefit*

This is one of the best-kept secrets in America!

The Veterans Administration's Aid and Attendance program provides qualified veterans and their surviving spouses income in addition to any pensions they receive, to pay for home care or assisted living care they may require. Veterans who meet the required service connection level can be living either in a private home or an assisted living facility. (Veterans in skilled nursing or rehab centers cannot receive this benefit.)

The program is based on various criteria, such as the following: the veteran must have served active duty during a war (it isn't necessary to have been deployed for combat), and must need assistance with at least one daily activity—eating, bathing, dressing, hygiene or so on, and provide written proof from a physician verifying that the assistance is needed.

This money is in addition to the veteran's service or disability pension, and any Social Security or other disability income the veteran receives. Aid and Attendance benefits are tax free, and indexed annually for inflation. The additional income—currently up to $2,120 monthly—can be instrumental in affording medical care in the home or the assisted living center.

Applications for the Aid and Attendance pension can be made on-line at the VA website. The website will also help locate the nearest Pension Management Center in your state, where assistance is offered at no charge in applying for this benefit. There are also companies that, for a fee, assist veterans and their families in applying for this program. Any elder law attorney would also be able to determine eligibility and help with the application process.

However, this benefit may not be paid without eligibility to a pension. A veteran may be eligible for Aid and Attendance when:

- The veteran requires the aid of another person in order to perform personal functions required in everyday living, such as bathing, feeding, dressing, attending to the wants of nature, adjusting prosthetic devices, or protecting himself or herself from the hazards of the daily environment; or the veteran is bedridden, in that the disability or disabilities require remaining in bed apart from any prescribed course of convalescence or treatment; or the veteran is a patient in a nursing home due to mental or physical incapacity.

- The veteran is blind, or so nearly blind as to have corrected visual acuity of 5/200 or less in both eyes, with concentric contraction of the visual field to 5 degrees or less.

Eligible wartime veterans must:

- Have served active duty during war time:
    o World War II—December 7, 1941 to December 31, 1946
    o Korean Conflict—June 27, 1950 to January 31, 1955
    o Vietnam Era—August 5, 1964 to May 7, 1975 (or February 28, 1961 for veterans who served "in country" before August 5, 1964)
    o Persian Gulf War—August 2, 1990 through a date to be set by law or presidential proclamation
- Received an honorable discharge
- Be 65 years old or older, or disabled
- Meet the VA Asset Limit
- Have limited income and/or have extensive un-reimbursed medical expenses

Once approved, eligible dependents are the veteran and one dependent; the veteran's surviving spouse will be entitled to assistance in his or her retirement.

Information and items needed to apply:

- Military Discharge Papers: DD-214.
- Married veterans and surviving spouses need to provide a copy of their marriage certificate.
- Surviving spouses need to provide a copy of the veteran's death certificate.

- Form VA 21-2680—Examination for Housebound status or permanent need for regular Aid and Attendance.
- A letter outlining monthly and annual fees paid to an assisted living community or home care agency.
- All financial statements.

*Housebound Benefits*

Like Aid and Attendance, Housebound benefits may not be paid without eligibility for pension. A veteran cannot receive both Aid and Attendance and Housebound benefits at the same time. A veteran may be eligible for Housebound benefits when:

- The veteran has a single permanent disability evaluated as 100 percent disabling and, due to such disability, is permanently and substantially confined to his or her immediate premises, or,
- The veteran has a single permanent disability evaluated as 100 percent disabling and another disability, or disabilities, evaluated as 60 percent or more disabling.

You may apply for Aid and Attendance or Housebound benefits by writing to the VA regional office having jurisdiction of the claim. That would be the same office where you filed a claim for pension benefits. If the regional office of jurisdiction is not known, you may file the request with any VA regional office.

You should include copies of any evidence, preferably a report from an attending physician validating the need for Aid and Attendance or Housebound type care. The report should be in sufficient detail to determine whether there is disease or injury producing physical or mental impairment, loss of coordination, or conditions affecting the ability to dress and undress, to feed oneself, to attend to sanitary needs, and to keep oneself ordinarily clean and presentable. In addition, it is necessary to determine whether the claimant is confined to the home or immediate premises.

Whether the claim is for Aid and Attendance or Housebound, the report should indicate how well the individual gets around, where the individual goes, and what he or she is able to do during a typical day.

*VA Hospitals and Medicare*

Even if a senior veteran has full access to a local VA hospital, he or she may still need to be on Medicare Part B to cover fees for physicians and procedures that may not be available through their local VA medical system.

Many seniors also qualify for their state's Medicaid program, which can offset any medical expenses should they need them while traveling, or for any procedure which the local VA medical system cannot provide for the veteran.

Local American Legions also host fundraisers for veterans who need assistance or are struggling financially. The local legions can be a great resource to additional programs the veteran qualifies for, as well as an excellent place to save money on food and drink.

An important reason to apply for benefits is that the government uses the total number of veterans who are approved for benefits as a baseline for allocating money for the healthcare programs. Even if a veteran decides not to use the VA healthcare system, having applied for benefits can still reserve a spot for a veteran in need in the future.

Resources

VA Home Page: www.va.gov

Veteran Benefits Info:
    benefits.va.gov/BENEFITS/factsheets.asp

Veterans Affairs—National Caregiver Support Line:
    1-855-260-3274

Military and Veteran Benefits: www.military.com

National Association of County Veteran Service Officers:
    www.nacvso.org

VA Caregiver Support: 1-866-260-3274 or
    www.caregiver.va.gov

Veterans Crisis Line: 1-800-273-TALK or
    www.veteranscrisisline.net

*Karyn Rizzo is a healthcare consultant and author. This chapter was adapted from her book* Aging in America: Navigating Our Healthcare System, *which is available at Amazon, Barnes & Noble, Kindle and Nook, and at www.agingguidebook1.com*

# Learning to Cope

You're braver than you believe,
and stronger than you seem,
and smarter than you think.
—A.A. Milne

*Linda Burhans*

## The Caregiver "AAA" Dilemma

Many times, as caregivers we think we're too selfish and often feel ashamed about it. But the truth is we get out of the habit of taking care of ourselves. Here's how it works: You find the whole thing almost impossibly hard, yet other caregivers seem to do it without complaining or giving up—so you think there must be something wrong with you, and you drive yourself on until you're ready to drop.

We didn't apply for our jobs as caregivers. We've had no training. We're not even sure if we are good at it. And on top of everything, we've got our own lives to lead.

Informal caregiving is a challenging yet rewarding experience. Understanding how to balance responsibilities by taking care of your needs and involving others helps manage the natural stress and isolation of being a caregiver.

In the past several years, I have facilitated more than 600 support groups and workshops for family caregivers. I always find a consistent, common thread. I call it the "AAA" Dilemma of Caregivers.

Caregivers do not Ask for help, they do not Accept help, and they do not Acknowledge themselves.

Many times caregivers are asked by a friend, neighbor or coworker, "Is there anything I can do to help you out?" And invariably the caregiver will say, "No, I'm okay."

But most of the time we are not okay. We definitely could

use some assistance. Usually it's just that we do not know how to answer. Then, when we keep saying no and not accepting help, people stop asking. For some reason many of us think that as caregivers it is our total responsibility to take sole care of our loved ones.

I suggest this: take a little time to sit down and write a list of some things with which you can accept help. Then the next time your friend or neighbor asks if there is a way they can help, you can pull out your list. It doesn't have to be something directly related to caregiving. Perhaps ask them to mow your lawn, pick up some groceries, or come over to do a load of laundry and visit a bit while you're busy with another task?

I guarantee they will be delighted to help you. That's why they have been asking!

One woman emailed me after attending one of my workshops. She said she thought about what I had said and decided to make a list. She only put one thing on her "list"—if someone could come over any afternoon between 2 and 4 p.m. and let her take a nap, that would be just wonderful. Her exact words were, "And I am pleased as punch to tell you that I am now napping seven days a week and my husband is getting seven different visitors who had stopped coming." Wow! What a world of relief she and her husband enjoy because she made one simple request.

So I strongly encourage all caregivers today to
*A*sk for help,
*A*ccept help, and
*A*cknowledge yourselves. You are not alone! There is help—all you have to do is realize that you, too, are cared about.

*Heidi Crockett*

## Optimal Mental Health for Caregivers

I often hear the question, "What can I do to reduce the effects of caregiver stress on my mental health?" If you haven't reached the point of asking, the time will come when stress will affect you. It's never too early—or too late—to take care of yourself and treat yourself as compassionately as you treat your loved one.

Caregiving leads to increased stress. It simply does. This increased stress is possibly the very reason why you are reading this book right now—maybe you're wondering what you can do about the overwhelming feelings you're grappling with as a caregiver? Perhaps you hope that gaining more information will comfort and calm your spirit.

Health studies on caregivers show that "prolonged exposure to the chronic stress of caregiving…predispose caregivers to hypertension and cardiovascular disease."[1] In other words, you're more likely to develop high blood pressure after having been a caregiver. This chapter is intended to provide you with tips for dealing with stress so that you can prevent these negative, long-term health effects of caregiver stress.

We'll begin by defining optimal mental health using Dr. Daniel J. Siegel's Triangle of Well-Being, referred to as the Wellness Triangle throughout the chapter. The concepts contained in this triangle diagram are derived from research in relational neuroscience. Through reviewing the three tips of this triangle, you'll learn that while some of the effects of stress are inevitable, most can be redirected in healthy ways and transformed. (To learn more about relational neuroscience and how to transform your stress, see the book version of this chapter, *Caregiver Stress: Neurobiology to the Rescue.*)

*Optimal Mental Health*

Take a moment and **write down your definition of optimal mental health.** If you have a journal or want to start a journal, I'd suggest using it to answer the questions that I ask in bold throughout the chapter.

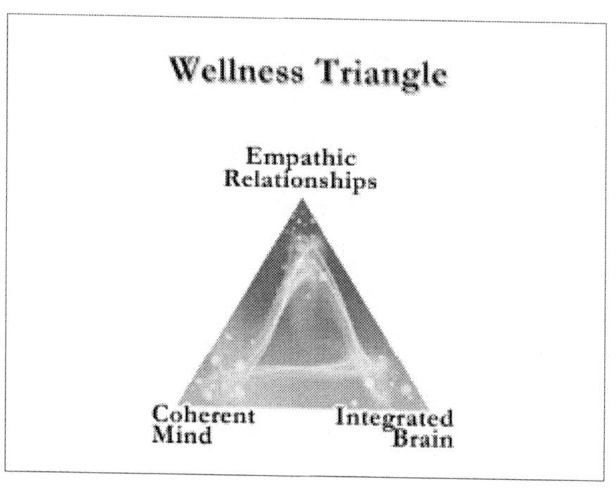


According to the Wellness Triangle, if you have "optimal mental health," all three tips of the triangle are optimally functioning so you have life balance and quality in your:

- real world, empathic relationships

- relationship with your mind and thoughts

- physical integration between and inside the different parts of your brain 2

Take a moment and think about how you fit in with the Wellness Triangle.

*Empathic Relationships Tip of the Wellness Triangle*

Think of your relationships with friends, family, and any people you love. Do you have relationships where you feel connected and validated? Are your needs—to be listened to and touched—being met? **Take some time to write about the important people you have in your life. Write about how you are grateful for these special people and about what they bring to your life.**

When someone gives us time, presence, love, and attention, it is like nourishment to our mental health—and our soul. High-quality interpersonal relationships occur when we feel we have the loving presence and attention of another: they are vital to our mental health. Studies show that recipients of affectionate communication are at less risk for physical illness and are prone to exhibit an enhanced ability to heal from the effects of illness or injuries.[3] In other words, high-quality interpersonal interactions are healing to the body.

Stella Resnick PhD, a well-known researcher on the subject of love, writes that during intimacy, "Your hearts are entrained and actually begin to beat in rhythm."[4] Next, the hormonal, immune, and respiratory systems align. Countless benefits such as decreased anger, anxiety, and depression occur with increased intimacy and connection. If you used to be in a reciprocal relationship with your spouse but are now primarily in a caregiving relationship, remember how important it is to find these nourishing "foods" of affectionate communication and intimacy. Be sure that you are filling in the gaps of what you have lost, either by strengthening existing connections with friends and family and/or making new connections.

If, however, a relationship isn't meeting your needs, do you have the ability to set boundaries, to say "no," or otherwise distance yourself from the person? **Take some time to write about the people you find it harder to say no to. What can you do to make it easier for you to say no?**

It goes without saying that the person you are caregiving is likely the hardest person to say no to and set healthy boundaries with, especially as they lose more mental and physical functioning. Everyone's needs are different. Don't compare yourself to others. When I was caregiving my husband, Roger, I reached the point of breakdown; I had to move out for two months and hire a live-in caregiver. I took care of my husband for eight hours each day, and then retreated to my rented room two blocks away. I moved through intense feelings of guilt and failure during that time, but I did what I had to do for myself. (See a list of helpful affirmations in *Caregiver Stress: Neurobiology to the Rescue*, the book version of this chapter.)

Caregiving for Roger was the hardest thing I have ever done. Like many caregivers, I obtained an injury (to my right wrist) and didn't seek medical attention until after he passed away. You must try to do your best to care for yourself and to ask for help, over and over, even when others say no and you feel uncomfortable asking.

Practice making and strengthening your empathic relationships at a time when you most need them. Now is when you find out who your friends truly are. If you feel alone and isolated, join a local support group. Reach out and connect. Someone else may need to hear exactly what you are going through, and you'll surely realize you are not as alone as you feel you are.


*Coherent Mind Tip of the Wellness Triangle*

**What is your relationship with your thoughts?** Do you constantly have thoughts and/or words racing in your brain?

What activities do you involve yourself in that help balance and ground you? What activities help decrease racing thoughts? What can you do to calm your central nervous system when you are experiencing increased anxiety?

How you answer this last question about calming your nervous system is at the crux of learning how to manage caregiver stress in healthy ways. As a frame of reference for what I mean when I write "coherent mind," I use the word "mind" to refer to the part of your awareness that is able to focus attention. Exercise, a good night's sleep, and adequate hydration are essential building blocks to creating a calm(er) mind. More suggestions on activities to help regulate and calm the mind are provided below.

When we are under stress and we use our mind to focus our attention in meditation, we can calm the over-firing of the limbic brain, and heal the body. Dr. Siegel notes some of the health benefits of meditation: "Recent studies of mindful awareness practices reveal that it can result in profound improvements in a range of physiological, mental, and interpersonal domains. Cardiac, endocrine, and immune functions are improved with mindful practices."[5]

To strengthen the coherent mind tip of the Wellness Triangle, consider introducing or increasing the amount of mindfulness practices in your life—such as meditation, chanting, QiGong, Tai Chi, yoga, or connected breathing. Get curious and have fun finding a practice that suits you.

*Integrated Brain Tip of the Wellness Triangle*

For the remainder of this chapter I'm going to focus on the integrated brain tip of the Wellness Triangle. Before I write some journal/self-reflection questions to consider on this tip, I will outline some brain basics and what happens in the brain when there is stress.

*The Brain*

The brain has lovingly been called "the most impenetrable treasure chest."[6] At 86 billion neurons and counting, I believe the brain is a miracle treasure chest.[7]

In the past, scientists thought that brain growth stopped by age twenty-five. Modern neuroscience has shown that the ability of new nerves to form (called neurogenesis) and to make new connections with each other (known as neuroplasticity) is possible throughout the human lifespan. All this new scientific understanding of brain health is great news for adults at any age. Neuroplasticity and neurogenesis prove you can teach an old dog new tricks. Here is one example: Dr. Siegel describes an inspiring case study of a ninety-three-year-old man who uses mindfulness techniques to grow and transform his brain. "As he approached his ninety-fourth birthday, Stuart sent me a note: 'I cannot tell you how much fun I am having. Life has new meaning now. Thank you.' I thank him for teaching me, for teaching all of us, how resilient our integrative brains can be."[8]

So, modern research has demonstrated how neuroplasticity, neurogenesis, and our brain's resiliency can help us appreciate that we can literally alter our own minds, in order to best deal with stress.

### The Triune Brain

Neuroscientists have developed a model to describe our brains based on three parts that are referred to collectively as the triune brain. The three parts of the triune brain are the brain stem, the limbic brain, and the prefrontal cortex.[9]

The brain stem, which connects the base of the brain to the spinal cord, is also known as the "reptilian brain." It is the oldest part of the brain and controls basic functioning such breathing, heart rate, blood pressure, and swallowing.

The limbic brain, also called the limbic system, is a collection of structures that operate by influencing the endocrine system and the autonomic nervous system. Think of the middle-inside of your brain as the general location for the limbic brain. While I won't name all the structures, you might have heard of the amygdala, the hypothalamus, and the hippocampus as being parts of it. What's most important to know about the limbic brain is that your emotional life is largely housed here, and it has a great deal to do with the formation of memories. The fight-flight-freeze mode comes primarily from the limbic brain.

Completing the triune brain is the prefrontal cortex, sometimes called the neocortex. This region of the frontal cortex, at the very front of the brain (located in your general forehead area), is involved in problem-solving and complex thought. Some functions of the prefrontal cortex include morality, intuition, higher reasoning, and fear modulation— the ability to unlearn a fear. The prefrontal cortex is basically the part of the brain that thinks about thinking. I'm asking you to use it to think through the concepts in this chapter and apply them in your life. Maybe take a moment and massage your forehead while thanking your amazing prefrontal cortex!

*The Brain and Stress*

When you are experiencing stress, the limbic brain is firing (think "fight, flight, freeze mode") and the prefrontal cortex, where executive functioning and higher reasoning occur, is off-line. (Remember, the prefrontal cortex of the brain, around the area of your forehead, is where executive functioning and higher reasoning occur while the limbic brain controls our instinctual reactions.) This is the reason why counselors teach hostile couples self-calming techniques for when their conversations become too heated: their prefrontal cortexes are off-line and, consequently, they are not going to be capable of having much empathy and higher reasoning.

Whenever you are feeling emotionally charged, agitated,

or "on edge," practice breath awareness, prayer, and other self-calming techniques. This is when strengthening the coherent mind tip pays off. Mindfulness and breath awareness activities keep the body's stress response from taking over executive functioning. (There are many good and brief meditation videos for free on the Internet. A great starting point is singing the "Sa Ta Na Ma" meditation by Snatam Kaur while tapping your fingers to your thumb.)

*Brain Integration*

Now that we have explored the triune brain and the limbic brain vs. the prefrontal cortex, let's return to the brain integration tip of the Wellness Triangle. In the diagram, brain integration is defined as having balance and quality in the physical integration between and inside the different parts of your brain.

Studies show that new challenges—learning a new musical instrument or language, even driving a different route from home to the doctor—help increase neurogenesis and neuroplasticity. There are physical therapy-like brain exercise programs like the Brain Fitness Centers of Florida that strengthen your brain. Also, current brain research is showing that frequent social interaction is vital for preventing cognitive decline.

Physical exercise that increases your heart rate—even walking, is fantastic for your brain health, as well as your overall physical health. Exercise is one of the few clinically proven methods to reduce the effects of stress and depression, and lab studies have shown that exercise can increase the rate of neurogenesis, even in aging.

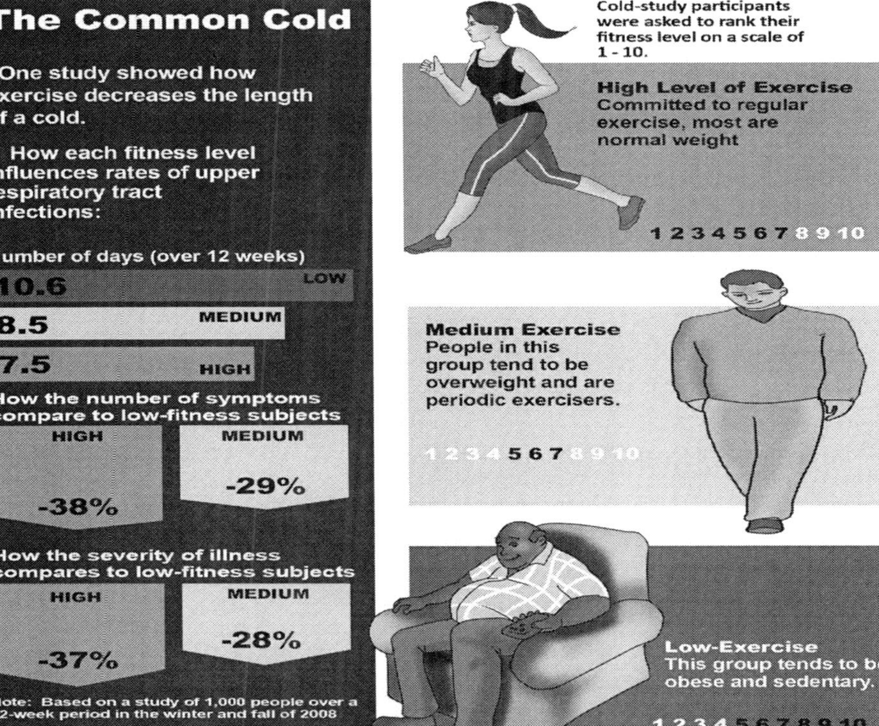

The Common Cold
One study showed how exercise decreases the length of a cold.
How each fitness level influences rates of upper respiratory tract infections:
Number of days (over 12 weeks)
10.6 LOW
8.5 MEDIUM
7.5 HIGH
How the number of symptoms compare to low-fitness subjects
HIGH -38%
MEDIUM -29%
How the severity of illness compares to low-fitness subjects
HIGH -37%
MEDIUM -28%
Note: Based on a study of 1,000 people over a 12-week period in the winter and fall of 2008
Source: Prof. David C. Nieman, Appaladashian State University
Cold-study participants were asked to rank their fitness level on a scale of 1 - 10.
High Level of Exercise
Committed to regular exercise, most are normal weight
1 2 3 4 5 6 7 8 9 10
Medium Exercise
People in this group tend to be overweight and are periodic exercisers.
1 2 3 4 5 6 7 8 9 10
Low-Exercise
This group tends to be obese and sedentary.
1 2 3 4 5 6 7 8 9 10
Other studies show that exercise...
Decreases depression as well as anti-depressant medication
Reduces the occurrence of hypertension by 40%
Lowers the risk of colon cancer by 60%
Reduces the risk of developing Alzheimer's disease by 40%
Reduces the occurrence of diabetes by 50%

1. **On a scale of 1 to 10, how do you rate your memory?** If you want a baseline, grab a timer and name as many animals as you can in one minute. Do this test once a year. If you name fourteen or fewer animals this indicates cognitive impairment. If you are concerned about your memory, please follow up with a neurologist.

2. **Out of the tips listed above that help improve brain integration—new challenges, exercise, and brain games, and activities, write one new activity you are willing to try. When?**

3. **When you are under high levels of stress such as a crisis, what can you do to help remember that the limbic system is firing and the prefrontal cortex—and higher reasoning—is off-line?**

I am asking this last question for after you've dealt with the initial mandatory concerns of a crisis. Some of my suggestions for question No. 3 are: having one of your close friends act as an "emergency buddy" you can call, who also has read this chapter and can remind you; having a visual reminder on the fridge; having a "safe zone" in your house where you can go to shut off your brain for a few minutes (or hours) while the fight-flight-freeze mode calms down. And simply remind yourself that, when you are extremely stressed out and anyone wants you to make a complex decision that requires a fully functioning prefrontal cortex, it's okay to say, "Let me get back to you on that."

I believe the limbic brain vs. prefrontal cortex is one reason why someone who has just lost a spouse is encouraged to not make any major decisions for at least one year. The intensity of grief clouds the functioning of the prefrontal cortex after the death (or any major trauma).

Again, every circumstance is different. If you have been

experiencing anticipatory grief as a caregiver, such as when a loved one is given a terminal diagnosis, the ability to make clear decisions after a loss might come back sooner. I decided to go back to graduate school for social work just five months after my husband passed away. It took another nine months before I was attending classes but that decision, and the following focus required to carry it through, was one of the smartest decisions I have ever made.[10]

The social work program I enrolled in surrounded me with caring people, so that I felt connected (empathic relationships tip of the Wellness Triangle), and this gave my life meaning and purpose. Meaning and purpose are vital parts of mental health. If you are weighed down by the responsibilities of caregiving, it is important for your brain integration to hold tight to activities that make your life meaningful.

Personally, I went through a long phase while caregiving where I felt that life was meaningless. I had been full of positivity and very Pollyannaish as a young adult and needed to come to terms with the fact that life can feel extremely meaningless, especially in the face of devastating news. Studies show that successful grief resolution involves how we make meaning out of our circumstances. Grieving and grief resolution, as well as meaning-making, all require the prefrontal cortex and are important elements in brain integration.

When someone dies, your memory of them is literally stored in the neural pathways in your brain. When you mourn their death, you are physically retracing those neural pathways. Deciding what the sadness means in the greater picture of your life is important to integrating those memories in your brain, as opposed to them being shelved away and denied. Dr. Siegel writes, "When we block our awareness of feelings, they continue to affect us anyway. Research has shown repeatedly that even without conscious awareness, neural input from the internal world of body and emotion influences our reasoning and decision-making…in other words, you can run but you cannot hide."[11] Perhaps knowing that you cannot hide will help bring strength to your caregiving journey, to embrace the gamut of emotions inherently involved with grief and anticipatory grief.

My experience with grief was that it was like cloudy weather—it would eventually pass, but until then I had to sit with it and feel it. Many times in the last year my husband lived and during the year after he died I only wanted to be alone in nature or with other widows or widowers. I encourage you to embrace what you need without judgment in every phase of caregiving.

Remember the three tips of the Wellness Triangle— empathic relationships, coherent mind, and an integrated brain—and know that all three are vital for optimal mental health. Making consistent efforts to reduce stress will not only make you a better caregiver, it will ensure the likelihood of your having good physical health far into the future.

*Endnotes*

1   Shaw, William S., et al. "Longitudinal analysis of multiple indicators of health decline among spousal caregivers." Annals of Behavioral Medicine 19.2 (1997): 107.

2   For those interested in more about the triangle, I recommend Dr. Siegel's book, *Mindsight*, which I quote three times in this chapter.

3   Floyd et al., 2007; Schwartz & Russek 1998; Floyd & Morman 2000.

4   Resnick, S. (2012). *The Heart of Desire Keys to the Pleasure of Love*. New Jersey: John Wiley & Sons, Inc., 124.

5   Siegel, D. (2006). "An Interpersonal Neurobiology Approach to Psychotherapy. "Psychiatric Annals, 36(4), 250.

6   Lewis T., Amini F. and Lannon R., *A General Theory of Love*. New York: Random House (2000). p.6

7   Azevedo, F., et al. "Equal numbers of neuronal and nonneuronal cells

make the human brain an isometrically scaled-up primate brain." J Comp Neurol. 513.5 (2009): 532-41.

8    Siegel, D. (2010). *Mindsight*. New York: Random House: p.119.

9    The brain stem, limbic system, and neocortex are technically called "the reptilian complex, paleomammalian brain, and the neomammalian complex" in Paul D. MacLean's triune brain concept.

10  My personal philosophy is if I am feeling crappy at a certain point in my life anyway, to go ahead and do something that will be good for my long-term, financial well-being. What I've found is that at the bare minimum, I'm still feeling crappy doing whatever it is I've committed to doing, (e.g. going back to school) but then I finish and I have both increased self-confidence because I completed that task and increased social capital, such as a degree, so that I have more job opportunities. (Doing this is another example of brain integration: I use my prefrontal cortex to think about my circumstance and to choose activity despite strong emotions, likely coming from my reactive, limbic brain.)

11  Siegel, D. *Mindsight*. New York: Random House (2010): p.125

*Heidi Crockett, LCSW, CMC, CSE is an AASECT-certified, professional speaker on stress reduction, brain health, and intimacy. She provides counseling as a Licensed Clinical Social Worker. She is author of* Caregiver Stress: Neurobiology to the Rescue, *the workbook version of this chapter about how to transform your stress. For more information, visit www.HeidiCrockett.com*

*Linda Burhans*

## How a Little Boy Changed an Elderly Man's Life

I often speak to youth groups about random acts of kindness. About a year or so ago I spoke to a wonderful group of energetic children. When I finished speaking, one of the teachers pulled me over to the side.

"Linda, see that little boy over there? Michael is a wonderful young man. Although his parents hold down three jobs, they are still very poor. He is the oldest of three children and has a lot of responsibility with his brother and sister. He cooks for them every evening and helps them with their homework. He, however, continues to struggle with his reading. We need to find a way we can help this boy."

I had facilitated a support group the day before. A woman in the group had cried the entire time. She said her husband, a retired English teacher, was confined to a bed and he felt hopeless.

The light bulb went off!

I met with the elderly man the next day. I told him of the young boy who was struggling in reading, and asked if Michael could come and read to him twice a week.

"I guess so," he whispered.

I then met with Michael. I told him there was an elderly man who was very lonely and wondered if Michael could go and read to him twice a week.

"I would love to do that!" he said with enthusiasm.

About two months later I received a call from the woman.

She calls her husband Mr. Ornery.

"I have to tell you, Linda, on the days that Michael comes to read, Mr. Ornery is happy from the moment he opens his eyes until the moment he closes them in the evening."

The next week I ran into Michael at the supermarket and he asked me, "Did they have milk boxes outside your house when you were a kid?"

"Yes, they did," I responded with a chuckle.

At the end of the school year I learned that Michael's reading grade went from a D to an A. He also was learning history that will be lost if we don't speak to our elders.

And Mr. Ornery was happy at least two days a week.

A few months later, Mr. Ornery and his wife decided to move back to their hometown, over 3000 miles away, to be closer to their family.

Michael and Mr. Ornery continue to read and chat together—via Skype.

Then the wife called me, to say she was absolutely delighted and not calling her husband "Mr. Ornery" anymore. "Linda, Mr. Happy now has seven children who read to him. Two of them call him grandpa because they never had a grandfather. Although he is confined to that bed, I have not seen him this happy in many years! His love for these children has changed our lives."

Need I say I was thrilled, and that I shed a few tears of gratitude?

*Mary Jane Cronin*

# How Can Journal Writing and Support Groups Help Me as a Caregiver?

Being a caregiver can fill you with emotions that are both positive and negative. There is a sense of pride and accomplishment in providing care for someone who may have taken care of you. There may be the comfort of knowing your parent or spouse is secure in your home. There also may be unpleasant emotions, such as anger, because you have had to put your life on hold to care for someone else. There may be envy of siblings who live far away and cannot take on the task of providing care. All of these emotions are common and normal when taking on the care of someone else.

Journal writing is a helpful way to put your feelings to words and to help understand why you feel the way you do. As you, the writer, begin to put words on the paper, there is flow of energy that travels from the heart to the brain. Thoughts are formed into words, which then flow from the brain through your hand and finally to the page.

Journaling provides a safe place to express those feelings held inside your heart. It can give you an opportunity to clarify what you are thinking and feeling. Writing can help you begin to soften some turbulent emotions, such as anger or resentment. Holding these emotions inside may delay acceptance about taking on the task of caregiving. Writing can give you time to better understand both your emotions and the feelings that must follow.

Healing through writing occurs not from being perfect or re-reading one's words. Healing begins by getting one's thoughts out of the heart and mind in the first place. Don't feel the need to rush your writing. It may begin as a few lines on day one, and blossom into a few pages once you feel comfortable with the process.

Physical, emotional, and spiritual pain can all be reduced through journaling. Some of the benefits of journaling include:

- Helping you work through issues that are difficult to communicate in other ways.
- Offering a personal, private, and confidential way to sort out your feelings.
- Providing you an outlet to express your feelings and needs when they are the strongest.

Allow yourself some alone time, maybe fifteen minutes at first. Sit in a quiet place with paper and pen. Do not worry about what you are writing—it is only for you. Don't worry about the grammar or punctuation. Think of it as "free-writing," where your mind is guiding your hand that's holding the pen. This exercise allows you to unclutter your mind of those thoughts you have been carrying around, of those feelings you have been unable to share with another person because you think they would never understand. Share with your journal what you think and feel during these quiet times. If you get angry or tears start to fill your eyes, allow those feelings to surface and write how you feel about having this happen.

We cannot keep ourselves filled with emotions and thoughts without bursting—and those burst episodes often happen at the wrong time and place, such as verbally lashing out at your loved one has soiled himself or spilled food on the clean clothes that you just helped her put on. These types of outbursts can cause friction and unhappiness in the household. You know you were not really mad at them, you were just spent or worn-out. Feeling overwhelmed and speaking harshly at your own children who are just "being kids" can result in resentment now that their grandparent is living in their home.

When you write in your journal about your concerns, you begin to find solutions to your problems. Dr. James W. Pennebaker made a discovery when he asked people to write down their deepest feelings about an emotional upheaval they had experienced in their lives. In his book Opening Up, Pennebaker writes: "An emotional upheaval such as the life changing illness or change of roles touches every part of someone's life." Relationships with others are challenged, our self-esteem is shaken, and often our financial security is jeopardized. These events can result in rethinking one's feelings regarding issues of life and death. Writing helps us focus and organize these experiences.

In a famous experiment that dramatically altered understanding of the value of journaling, Pennebaker conducted studies with two sets of college students. He asked them to spend fifteen minutes a day for four consecutive days writing about a traumatic time in their lives. He had the first set of students write "just the facts" about had gone wrong. The second group was asked to not only include the facts, but to write how they felt about these events. At the end of the study, students who wrote both the facts and their emotions were missing fewer classes, had better grades, and were, overall, medically healthier. Their blood pressure and heart rates were lower and they reported having less trouble sleeping.

This may seem a bit excessive, but stress plays a role in all your body components. Journaling helped the students physically, in that they were less stressed after putting their feelings on paper. Emotionally, they were able to release their pent-up feelings to the paper and deal with them calmly. Cognitively, they were able to develop strategies to resolve the issues they wrote about in the pages of their journal.

Journal writing began for me following the loss of my son. Sitting at the computer alone at night, I would write letters to Heaven telling him what was happening after he left us. I listened to his favorite music with the computer's speakers turned up loud—the same music I must have told him 100 times to turn down. I cried at the injustice of his being taken from my life when he was sixteen. I remembered the fun times we had as a family and I would write of them, and of new memories we were forced to create without him. The writing allowed me to shed silent tears when I was trying to appear so strong on the outside for my other children. The writing helped me talk about the day he was given to me and the day he was taken away. The writing helped me heal.

What if you don't know how to get started or what to write? Here are three writing prompts to get you started.

- Tell me about your loved one.
- What is the hardest part of caregiving?
- What would I like my family and friends to know?

As a caregiver, journaling can help you sort out your feelings and begin to make future plans and memories to share with your loved one before they become too ill to enjoy them. The journal is your friend when your mind swims around endlessly on those rainy nights or as the house gently sleeps. When thoughts run through your head as you try to figure out how to juggle everything that the next day has in store for you, the journal is your inward support system.

But it also helps to talk to others who, like you, may have had to alter their lives to become caregivers. Caregiving groups are your outward support to help with your needs and emotions. Many caregivers who take on the role of caring for a parent, grandparent, or even a spouse begin to feel isolated. Often too tired to do anything other than what is needed, they may feel they are alone in this journey.

The truth is you're not alone. Churches, assisted living facilities, and even the homes of caregivers themselves have been offering gatherings or support groups for many years. They have seen the benefit of working jointly to deal with the many unknown and often frightening aspects of being a caregiver.

Attending a support group can be a bit worrisome for many caregivers. Even though it seems you have no time for a support group, that's when it is even more important for you to attend. Other men and women in your support group will understand what you are feeling. They can share your frustration at how much you, and your care receiver, are hurt by the inability of some family members and friends to offer you any help. Many of those in the support group have struggled to remain patient with some of their care receiver's behaviors, and they know how frustrating it can be trying to "navigate the system" to get affordable assistance.

If you are attending support group meetings, you are also likely to hear about caregiver workshops that might provide further support. Focusing on specific topics, such as getting Medicare or Medicaid or learning about advanced directives, these workshops will be filled with other caregivers who also will give you the outward support to continue providing care to your loved one.

Sometimes you need to reach out for help. This help may be found in a support group. Your first thought may be "I've got family and friends to help me." But ask yourself whether they really understand what you're up against? Your doctor, social worker, or counselor may be there for you, but you may need more. A mutual support group is a caring, open, and accepting environment for people just like you, who face similar ordeals and challenges. You come together to express common concerns and issues and provide and receive emotional support.

There are three types of support groups:

- Emotional growth and wellness groups are designed to improve overall health and well being, such as losing weight or, in these economic times, support in looking for work.

- Situational crisis groups are temporary meetings to help you through a difficult period, such as a parent's death.

- Chronic illness/conditions groups are developed to help one cope with a long-term physical, mental, emotional, or social issue. This illness could be your own or that of someone close to you, such as cancer, dementia, Parkinson's disease, muscular sclerosis, or Alzheimer's disease.

These meetings may last an hour or two and may follow an agenda or may remain spontaneous. Some groups meet for a limited time, others indefinitely. Most are free or charge only a minimal fee to pay for meeting space.

Some of the support groups offer a place for your loved one to wait while you attend the meeting. If this is not the case, asking a friend or family member to stay with your loved one for that time will be beneficial to you.

Newcomers to support groups often feel out of place in the initial meetings. When you begin attending you may at first want to just listen to others; later, you may want to share your own story. These meetings are a great place to just sit and listen. Participation is voluntary and just being able to hear how someone else is managing a situation similar to your own can be very helpful. Most groups focus on sharing their experiences in order to give others an opportunity to gain some knowledge about the reasons that brought them to the group.

Support groups may provide information or offer advice, but that is not their main purpose. They are about sharing the strength and hopes that are needed in this position, which can often be difficult. Some of the benefits you get from attending a support group are:

- Information you may not have known about, regarding being a caregiver or the specific illness your loved one is dealing with.

- People who will empathize with you about your situation. Family and friends may attempt to be supportive, but if they have not "lived it" they may not understand what you are going through.

- Help with informational websites and "navigating the system" sources you may not have needed to know about until becoming a caregiver.

- News about community workshops in your area where you can gather additional information.

Feelings of anger and guilt, if left to fester, can numb you to the needs of your loved one. Becoming apathetic about their care could cause you to miss something crucial. Attending a support group with others who have been in those situations lets you know you are not alone and gives you permission to express those feelings, as well as a chance to hear about ways they were able to resolve them.

You need to make sure you're not socially isolated and this is where support groups can help. One of the great aspects of the caregiving burden that leads to depression isn't from the hours spent giving care—it's from the caregiver feeling deprived of their own time. You really need to take time for yourself, whether it's going inward and writing in a journal or extending outward and finding a support group that can assist you as you travel this journey of caregiving.


*Mary Jane Cronin, LMHC, is a national speaker, international author, and an expert on the benefits of journaling and self-care. For more information, visit www.cronincounseling.com*

*Linda Burhans*

## Acknowledging Your Loved One's Feelings

One Saturday morning a woman by the name of Marie came to my support group. She was the only person who came that day, but, as I always say, "Whoever is supposed to be there, will be."

The woman was distraught. Her mother had recently passed away and she had moved to Florida to care for her dad, who was a really angry man. Her parents had moved here from Georgia only three months earlier and her mom died shortly after, very unexpectedly. She herself was single and experiencing some financial problems, so her brothers and sisters figured it would be best for her to move in and take care of their dad. (I call these women the "designated daughters.") She had never even visited Florida before and was confused and lonely, with no knowledge of the area or resources.

We talked for almost two hours that day and she became a regular at my support groups and workshops. A few months later, she phoned me. "I have a story to tell you, Linda, and I am so excited."

Recently one of her sisters had come to visit and she was very surprised to see how well her sister was adjusting to her new role as caregiver. "You look wonderful!" her sister exclaimed. "What are you doing?"

"I have been attending some support groups and workshops for caregivers," Marie answered. "Through them I have also been able to find out about resources for Dad. They told me that I need to take care of myself if I am going to be able to take care of him, so one of the things I do is go for a one hour walk every day. I don't care if it is hot or even raining. I make sure I go for my walk."

Her dad, sitting in his wheelchair, scowled and said, "Well, isn't that good for you! It's nice somebody can walk!"

Her sister replied, "I came here to have a nice visit and if you are going to be so negative, Dad, then we are going to talk in the other room."

"Go ahead, I don't care!" he replied.

The sisters went into the next room but Dad kept listening.

"One of the best things I have been doing is attending a caregiver journaling group," Marie said. "I can get my feelings out in a non-judgmental way. I can share if I want to or I can keep it to myself."

With that, Dad yelled from the other room, "It's great, someone around here can get their feelings out!"

"Dad, we are here to help you in any way we can," the sisters said in unison as they went to their dad's side.

"Do you think you would like to journal?" Marie asked him.

"Maybe," he replied.

They gave him a black-and-white notebook. About an hour later he wrote down one sentence. Three hours later he scribbled another sentence. He did this on and off for three days. On the fourth day he handed them the book. "Here, now you can see how I feel!"

The sisters open the book and read, "I am so tired. I am

so tired of being a burden to my family. I am so tired of taking so many pills. I am so tired of not being able to go out. I am so tired of not being able to eat what I want..."

The sisters felt heartbroken. "Dad, you're not a burden to us," Marie's sister said. "You held down three jobs when we were kids to keep food on the table. We want to take care of you in any way we can."

"Maybe you are taking too many pills," Marie added. "We will go to the doctors with you and see what we can do about this."

The sisters went through the entire list, acknowledging every one of their dad's feelings.

"Things have been so much better with Dad since then, Linda," Marie told me. "In fact, he would like to know if he can come to your next journaling workshop."

I was jumping for joy. "Sure, bring him next week."

The next week Marie pushed her ninety-year-old dad, Joe, in his wheelchair into the group. He was beaming. He shared with the group his first journal entries and then proceeded to share his new ones.

"I am so glad I have a family that loves and cares for me. I am so glad I am not taking as many pills. I am so glad that when Marie goes for her walk I can join her."

Yipeeeeeee!

Joe is now writing short stories about his childhood. His family loves hearing his stories and sharing with him.

Please do not forget to acknowledge the feelings of your loved one! I guarantee it will make your caregiving journey more joyful.

*P.S. Joe is Italian and from Brooklyn and he brought me the best meatballs I have ever eaten.*

*Paula Stahel*

## The Power of Story

"I can't wait to read what happens next!"

I had to laugh. "Maggie, this is your life story. You know what happened next."

"Yes, but then it was normal life. Now it's exciting."

At ninety-one, Maggie's mind was sharp, her body was failing. The year before she had to quit dancing at her beloved jazz events and now needed a wheelchair to attend them. She still lived independently but needed a walker to maneuver around her small, art-filled apartment and the retirement community building. She had hired me to compile her experiences as a WAC during World War II, so her grandchildren would know her as more than their grandmother. A career writer herself, she had journals, copies of her published articles, and hundreds of letters she'd sent home that were saved by her mother.

From the moment I delved into that archive, I dubbed her the female Forrest Gump of the Pacific Theater. Stationed in Papua New Guinea as a cryptographer, she and a friend started a monthly "newspaper" for service personnel. The two women were among the first in Manila, even before the male troops, when MacArthur re-took The Philippines. They broke the rules big time by hitchhiking to the front during a major battle, and she told me the true story behind the heavily censored version she wrote for a military publication. After VJ Day she became the first and only female and civilian reporter for *Pacific Stars and Stripes*, in post-war Japan. Later she turned down Uncle Sam's free ticket home and set off, alone, to journey back to the States. In Korea she jumped ship and hitched a ride to Seoul for a night of partying, and when she returned the ship the captain tossed her in the brig until he unloaded her in China. In Nepal she spent a day with the Dali Llama. In India a prince courted her. She arrived in Iran on the day Israel declared independence and war broke out. In Rome, the Swiss Guard, in full regalia on their white horses, delivered her an invitation to meet Pope Pious after she had dropped off a letter at the Vatican from a nun she'd met, who'd been the pope's first teacher. In Paris, working for the U.N., she handled Eleanor Roosevelt's correspondence, and acquired a poodle puppy that young Indira Gandhi insisted on walking every day. And that's barely scratching the surface of her experiences!

It had all seemed so normal to her then. All of our lives seem "normal" as we're living them. It's in the looking back that we realize our experiences were both unique and universal, and the stories we share with others reverberate because we all experience the same things: love, joy, loss, failure, success. And the lessons we learned along the way show others how to make their way, too.

As we approach advanced age we all wonder, "Did my life mean anything? Will I be remembered?" More than death itself, we fear the answer to those two questions will be no. We begin reminiscing about the past, looking for the themes of our lives.

Not that many years ago, this need to reminisce was considered a sign of incipient dementia. Now, it's widely recognized that life review is a stage as important to healthy development as childhood, adolescence, and maturity are. The need to remember our experiences helps us know that our lives have meaning. Being asked to tell our stories to a willing listener assures us we will be remembered.

"I spent considerable time interviewing my mother in preparation for writing *Wish You Well*," wrote author David Baldacci, "and it was an enlightening time for me. Most of us assume we know all there is to know about our parents. However, if you take the time to ask questions and actually listen to the answers, you may find there is still much to learn about people so close to you."

Taking the time to get your loved one's stories will have a dramatic impact on both of your lives, and create a legacy for generations to come. So, when every day is packed with to-dos that leave little time for anything but caregiving, how do you go about it?

One of two ways: You can schedule it as a social time that's shared with your loved one, or you can engage the services of a professional personal historian.

*The Do-It-Yourself Approach*

First, gather a few necessary tools. You'll want a reliable means of recording your loved one's stories. The best choice is a simple digital recording device that captures mp3 audio you can transfer to a computer. Small digital recorders are quite inexpensive and can be purchased on-line, at most major box stores, or any office supply store. On smart phones and tablets, there's an app for that—Google "digital recording apps" and you'll find a plethora to choose from.

Don't just hand the recording device to your loved one and ask him to talk into it while you're off doing other things. And don't try to get the stories on the fly: "Mom, I'm going to put the clothes the dryer. Keep talking, I can hear you." No. Sit down with your loved one. Give her your undivided attention. Being an engaged listener stimulates the storyteller to share more, and more deeply.

(Please don't buy one of those fill-in-your-life-story books. They're lovely, but intimidating—"What if I make a mistake?!"—and are as poor at drawing out stories as being handed a recorder and told to talk into it.)

Schedule time to sit down with your loved one. Plan time once a week to sit in an undisturbed place with only your loved one and the recording device. Sessions should last no longer than ninety minutes. There are numerous reasons—the most important is that the human brain is unable to sustain continued activity at an optimum level for longer than ninety minutes.

Ask open-ended questions. An open-ended question is one that can't be answered yes or no. A great way to get a story going is to say, "Tell me about __________" and fill in that blank. Be affirming, and ask follow-up questions: "It sounds like you really enjoyed that. What made it so much fun?" "That must have been hard. How did you get through it?"

Interviewing is different from conversation. In conversation, talk goes back and forth. You may have memories of your own about some of the experiences or people your loved one talks about. Do not contradict your loved one: "Oh, that's not the way it happened"—or interject your own opinions: "I can't believe you thought that!" The stories and memories you are hearing are that person's, and will differ from your own. As an interviewer, your role is to keep the stories flowing and simply listen.

Begin with questions about your loved one's earliest memories. Our childhood experiences, when everything we encountered seemed new or unusual, are the ones most deeply imprinted in our memories. Lead the way to introspection by asking questions like "How did you feel about that?" or "What did you think about that later?"

Don't interrupt stories you've heard before. Just because

you know those stories doesn't mean everyone else will.

Don't press if your loved one doesn't want to talk about certain things, things too painful. The horrors of war, abuse, the loss of a parent at an early age cause wounds your loved one may not want to re-open. Being forced to revisit traumatic events can have a devastating effect.

Also, don't try to get certain "types" of stories. Expect that men will tell stories focused on career and/or military experiences. You're not likely to get "feelings" out of the guys, especially members of the Greatest Generation. Yet it's the opposite with women. We are genetically programmed to attend to relationships—our families, our children, our friends, and that's what our stories tend to revolve around, even if we've worked or had careers.

If your loved one is still able and enjoys writing, consider enrolling him in a life-writers class. Libraries are beginning to offer such programs for free, usually on a monthly basis. Many colleges and universities have "life long learners" courses, and senior citizens centers may offer such classes. While there is a fee, it will be nominal. Plus, if you take your loved one to a class, she'll engage in social stimulation, and you'll have an hour or two to run errands—or go to the park for much needed relaxation of your own.

*Engage a Professional Personal Historian*

Hiring a skilled professional is not inexpensive, but the value far exceeds the investment, which can be shared by several family members, and provides additional benefits in the process.

Professional personal historians offer a variety of services, all of which start with getting the stories. Generally, you have three types of services to choose from: a video history, an audio history, or a printed product—from a transcript of the interviews to a beautifully produced book replete with photographs.

Recording a video history is the fastest, for both you and your loved one, as it is generally done in one session, plus an advance meeting with the videographer to discuss what you want to achieve. Editing will take some time, and photos and documents can be scanned to include. The benefit here is that you preserve both your loved one in appearance and in voice. However, many elders are reluctant because they don't want to be forever remembered as "old and wrinkly."

If your loved one is a natural-born storyteller, an audio history is an outstanding choice—preserving the inflection in his voice, the laughter that erupts during stories, her voice in song. When Linda Burhans asked me to preserve her mother's stories, it was immediately apparent that audio was the ideal format. We could have turned Jo McCauley's words into a book and it would have been a fine, but no way would it have captured her larger-than-life personality, her raucous sense of humor, or the sweet sound of her voice singing a favorite song. Once the recording sessions are done, usually several weeks, the personal historian will lightly edit the material to remove coughs, ums, false starts, and so on, resulting in a memories far deeper than Story Corps could ever deliver.

Producing a book takes the greatest amount of time. Creating a legacy book takes at least six months, and can take as much as two years, depending on the scope. The biggest advantage is that books will endure, whereas changing technologies may render audio or video recordings obsolete. The number of recording sessions will be approximately the same as for an audio history—generally eight to ten weekly sessions. Each recording is transcribed, and then the personal historian crafts the transcripts into a cohesive narrative. The storyteller will receive a draft to review and correct before the book is designed, printed, and bound.

Where do you find such a professional? The place to start is the Association of Personal Historians, which has members around the world, including in virtually every state in the U.S. Through its membership directory you'll be able to locate people who offer the services you're interested in. Talk to several before selecting someone. Definitely involve your loved one in this process, as the relationship between them must be based on their mutual trust.

One advantage of retaining a personal historian is that relationship. Your loved one be engaged in a structured social-type activity over several weeks, and will have "homework" to prepare for the next session—thinking back on stories and events to talk about. A second advantage is that, during the recording sessions, you will have time to do other things. Depending on your loved one's physical health, that might mean running errands, taking care of things around the house, or being able to take a much needed nap.

Engaging your loved one in a life review project can have literally profound effects. Several years ago a colleague, Kate, and I were chatting when she talked about an experience she'd had during the previous year. A man contacted her in a state of near panic. He wanted to hire her to get his father's life stories, immediately. Doctors had told the family that "Mr. Jones" had approximately six months left to live. For decades he'd been a business powerhouse. He'd been active in social and civic circles, and was noted for his involvement in prominent charities. Now, all that was over. He was in his early eighties and had numerous ailments. He was losing his eyesight. He was hard of hearing. He felt completely forgotten by the world. He was bedridden, and had lost the will to live. It was his steady decline, not the diagnosis of a terminal illness, that resulted in the doctors' prognosis. Knowing she faced a difficult deadline,

Kate moved heaven and earth to accomplish the task. Six months later she delivered the books and placed a hardbound copy in Mr. Jones's hands as he lay in bed. He clasped it to his chest and said, "This is my book. This is my life." Kate left that day grateful to have made him, and the family, happy in his dying days.

About a year later, Mr. Jones's son called. Kate expected to hear that his father had died some time before. Instead, she learned that not only was he alive, he was hale and hearty! Within a few days of receiving the book, Mr. Jones began getting out of bed. Soon he was leaving the house, and reconnecting with friends. Then he became active again in civic organizations, which were happy to have a man of his acumen offer his talents. Reviewing his life, having his story preserved in tangible form, had shown him he was more than "an old man everybody'd forgotten about," as he had put it.

In preserving our stories, we share more than what we did. We share who we are, how we were shaped, the values we hold and want to pass down. We discover how we touched others' lives and that we played a role, however small, in the course of human events. We realize that even if we didn't scale a mountain, win the Nobel Prize, or lead nations, yes, our lives do have meaning, and yes, we will be remembered.

*Paula Stahel is a writer, editor, book coach, writing teacher, and public speaker who has specialized in life stories and memoir for more than fifteen years. She is a past president of the Association of Personal Historians Inc., and author of* Listen Up! The Art of Interviewing for Personal History. *For more information visit Breath & Shadows Productions—www.breathandshadows.com*

*Karen Karle-Truman, Ph.D.*

## Have You Accepted the Things You Cannot Change and Changed the Things You Can?

We have all heard of the Serenity Prayer. It is one of the most powerful and yet simplest ideas known to generations. One line, "Accept the things you cannot change," may have to become your new mantra in the disease process that has taken your loved one hostage.

Turn this around and ask what you can change. Can you change the diagnosis from a vague "dementia" to a very specific type of dementia—vascular, Lewy Body, etc.—that may be treatable and have completely different options for medications?

What kind of assessment has the memory disorder clinic team done? What are the recommendations? This is a primary step on the journey, and with a really good tangible plan, you can make arrangements for adult day-care, help in the home, and/or Meals on Wheels.

Of primary importance: Have you made sure your loved one is safe? Are there bugs or other vermin in and around the house? Is food fresh or out of date? When was the refrigerator last cleaned out? Are their clothes clean and washed? Are they changing clothes and washing themselves? Are they taking their medications as prescribed? If your loved one lives alone, is the neighborhood safe? Are they going to let in strangers? Are they giving away money? Are they engaging in phone conversations with unsolicited callers?

Should they still be driving? Is the auto insurance paid? Are the license plate tags renewed and current? Are there bumps and dents on the auto that they have no explanation for?

What do income and assets look like? Have you had conversations that address these very specific important legal and financial issues?

Who do you trust? Who can be a backup person in case the primary caregiver gets sick or even dies first? As you know, or are learning, this is a job for the strong in heart. It cannot be someone who has too much responsibility in his or her own life already, and it should not be a person who is not financially secure or who may squander your loved one's assets.

Have you looked at the long-term nature of your loved one's disease? Can you make subtle changes now that will make a huge difference later? Have you started looking into what kind of communities would be ideal and affordable? What kind of payment options there are? Would it be better to move your loved one closer to you?

Have you started to attend support groups? Each group has different "characters" and it may take several attempts to find the right group for you, but the benefits will astound you. You will learn things you knew nothing about, and the group will allow you to both vent and come to see things in an entirely new way.

Was your loved one a veteran or the spouse of a veteran? If so, this can be a huge deal regarding the costs of future care needs, as financial assistance through Aid and Attendance benefits may help pay for assisted living.

Can you get your loved one's stories now? Can you record their personal histories? These precious memories will fade away and be lost forever. Preserve this part of family history.

Have you discussed final wishes? Having the conversations about preferences can relieve that guilt and burden on you. Not knowing what our loved ones prefer and what their last wishes are can put undue coulda-shoulda-wouldas on our shoulders. This will haunt us and we may relive it over and over. Find out, make some pre-plans, create a checklist of ideas to start the conversation and then go for it. Preface introducing the topic with a hug and a sincere "I really want to know so I do the right things. Please fill me in on what you would like to have in your final days and after you pass. It will make my choices easier to handle at that time."

You will never be the same after you experience caregiving with heart and soul. The path is full of twists and unexpected turns, but the special strength that comes from within is worth every tear shed. To help you understand, these are some special stories that I have experience along the caregiving journey.

Recently, my husband, Jeff, and I were at some beach shops—I am always on the lookout for flamingo items—and the lady who was helping us was very kind. When she asked me why I was looking for flamingos, we got to talking and I gave her one of my business cards. She immediately told us about her mother, whom she is caring for at home and who needs more services. I spoke with her about adult daycare, calling the Senior Helpline, getting more in-home services, and finding a support group for herself. She was stunned to hear the amount of help that was available and said she would immediately act on this information. We never know who will cross our paths and how we are supposed to support one another—this is one more experience of being in the right place at the right time for a caregiver under stress!

Knowledge is powerful stuff. We are sometimes simply amazed by how many resources and programs are ready to assist you on this journey. I received a note from a husband who had dutifully attended support group meetings over the past few years. His wife of almost fifty years had passed away recently. He said that after he goes through some necessary healing, sorting, and paperwork, he will gather new strength by seeking out a grief support group. He said that by attending our caregiver meetings he realized how much he did not know and how much he needed to learn in order to help himself, his family, and his friends. People just like you have already walked in your shoes and understand the deep emotional pain. We can lean on each other when we need to.

In our support groups we hear so many stories. Lately, safety issues are a big concern. One couple received a sample "pod" of laundry soap in the mail. The husband, who has Alzheimer's, went out to get the mail when his wife was out of the house for a short time. She came home to find him choking and foaming at the mouth. She called 911 and he had to be hospitalized to remove the soap from his system. He thought the laundry soap pod was a big piece of candy (just as many young children do), and the more he kept chewing it, the more trouble it caused. This episode finally convinced his wife that he needed more supervision than she could provide, and he is now in adult day-care—where he is thriving with his new "volunteer work."

Recently we were, once again, in the emergency room with my mother-in-law. We were there for ten hours. Jeff stayed with her while I went to the hospital cafeteria for a much-needed break. While I was sitting and just staring out the window, I could not help but hear the lady seated next to me talking on her cell phone. She was calling her loved one's community to tell them she would not be able to bring "Mary" back because she had been diagnosed with frontal-lobe dementia and now needed more skilled care. My ears perked up. When she finished the call, I introduced myself, explained that I could not help but overhear, and asked if she needed some information and support for this part of the journey. Well, the tears started and she could not get enough information. It is a good thing I carry a basic "dementia kit" of info in my purse! She promised to attend our groups and to visit the National Institute of Health website for the latest information on this diagnosis. The two of us actually had a thirty-minute one-on-one support group in the cafeteria, and we were hugging and crying within only a few minutes. The message here is to reach out to a stranger: they may need your advice and hand-holding more than you can imagine.

The challenge for you is, how can your life change? Are you making a difference for someone in your family? Are you accepting the things you cannot change? What can you do today to start making good things happen for family and strangers alike? To create that "spark" and celebrate the new you. Your family will thank you and will then look forward to doing as much as they can for you because you set such a high standard.

Did you know that every county in the United States is served by an agency on aging? Many states have different names for their agencies, so use the Internet to search "senior services agency on aging" to find the best information and programs for your area. Through them you'll find insurance help, chore services, medication assistance, and can help find hidden resources that make a huge difference for both us and our loved ones.

Resources

End of Life: Helping With Comfort and Care:
     http://amzn.to/27ds8Ct

Center for Loss & Life Transition: www.centerforloss.com

Alzheimer's Disease Education and Referral Center:
     www.nia.nih.gov/alzheimers

Alzheimer's Foundation of America: www.alzfdn.org/

Alzheimer's Research & Prevention Foundation:
     www.alzheimersprevention.org/research

New York Times: Alzheimer's Disease News & Features:
     http://nyti.ms/1U0WVOr

Family Caregiver Alliance: www.caregiver.org

YouTube—Memorybridge: Gladys Wilson and Naomi
     Feil: http://bit.ly/1yct1eK

*Karen Karle-Truman, Ph.D., is president and founder of Dementia Caregiver Resources, Inc. She began traveling the Alzheimer's path in 1959, when her grandmother was placed into a nursing home. She then witnessed her mother, several aunts, and uncles taken by this terrible mind-robbing disease. A noted authority and author, Karle-Truman is cited as one of the nation's top memory care experts by Assisted Living Today. Her book,* The Dementia Caregiver's Little Book of Hope, *is an Alzheimer's/dementia resource book with the National Institutes of Health. For more information visit www.dcrinc.org*

## Caregiver Clubhouse

After about a year of facilitating various support groups, a gentleman in one of them asked if we could start a group just for men. "In most of the groups I attend there are only one or two men but many women, and we men have some different issues, Linda," he said.

"We could do that," I answered.

"Do you think you'll be able to handle us?" he asked.

I chuckled. "I'll do my best!"

We decided to call the group Caregiver Clubhouse, and started meeting the week after. Five guys attended the meeting regularly for two years. Others floated in and out.

The five regulars had a lot in common. Each one had been married for more than sixty years, and each of their wives had Alzheimer's and were living in a memory community. They would all go to feed their wives lunch and dinner, and then go home alone and cry. They all came from a generation that really believed in their marriage vows and missed their wives desperately. They began to form bonds.

Then one day I arrived at our regular meeting place. There were a few new gentlemen that day but not one of my five regular guys showed up. I was very concerned, as this had never happened before.

As soon as the meeting ended I start calling, to find out

if they were okay and where they had been.

The first fellow I reached said, "Two of us went fishing together and three went golfing, because that is what you're always telling us to do, Linda!"

"That's great, but not on the day of our support group," I scolded.

"Okay, okay! We'll make sure we don't do that again," he said with a laugh.

When I hung up the phone I was the one who cried—with happiness. It had taken me two years to convince them to do something for themselves.

The best part of it is that they were all in the same "boat." They could talk about their wives and each one would get it, or they could decide not to talk about their troubles and that was just fine.

If you are feeling alone in your caregiving experience, find a support group. It can make a world of difference.

*Note: All five wives and two of these gentlemen have passed away now. But the remaining three are still close friends and continue to share their lives with each other.*

# Learning to Accept

People ask me why I still visit her every day
when she doesn't remember me anymore.
I tell them, "Because I still remember her."
—Dick Jones

## Dementia Awareness

What is dementia?
- Dementia is a collective term that describes the symptoms of individuals with different brain disorders or damage that affect their memory, language, and thinking.
- Alzheimer's disease is the most commonly known disorder under the dementia umbrella.

What are some potential signs of dementia?
- Memory changes that disrupt daily life
- Confusion and/or disorientation as to time and place
- Poor reasoning and/or impaired judgment
- Difficulty with or loss of communication skills
- Changes in mood or personality
- Inappropriate behavior
- Challenges in planning or solving problems
- Difficulty completing familiar tasks

How do I communicate with or help someone who has or may be showing signs of dementia?
- Identify yourself and let the person know you are here to help
- Call the person by name
- Use short, simple words and sentences

- Speak only when you are visible to the person and maintain eye contact
- Speak slowly and clearly
- Allow the person time to process what you are saying
- Ask one question at a time
- Give one-step directions
- Limit distractions, such as noise
- Be aware of your tone of voice and body language
- Give visual cues
- Be patient, flexible, and understanding

What should I not do when communicating with someone who has or may show signs of dementia?
- Correct or criticize
- Argue
- Talk loudly if they do not understand
- Talk as if the person is not there
- Look frustrated or mad
- Rush the person
- Use sarcasm or humor

Who do I call for help?
- In case of an emergency, always call 911
- The person's caregiver (if possible)
- Police or Fire Department

*Maria Winer is the owner of Maria's Adult Day Care in Seminole, Florida, and is president of the Florida Caregivers Network.*
*For more information visit www.MariaCares.com and www.FloridaCaregiversNetwork.org*

*Linda Burhans*

## Mary & Aunt Bevie—When the Roles Reversed

Mary had been attending one of my support groups for about six months. She was caring for her Aunt Bevie. Aunt Bevie's husband, Jim, had died three years earlier, after a long battle with COPD and lung cancer. Aunt Bevie was diagnosed with Alzheimer's about a year later.

One day Mary asked to meet with me alone. She said she wanted to tell me the real story of Aunt Bevie, and she has allowed me to share it with you.

"My mother gave birth to me at the age of seventeen. She was a drug user, single, and could not hold a job. Her parents kicked her out of the house when she told them she was pregnant. A friend's family took her in and let her sleep on their couch. She would cook and clean for them. The dad of the family did not know she was pregnant and when he found out he asked her to leave, as he was not comfortable with a young girl seven months pregnant living in his home. He told her she was a terrible example to his young daughters.

"She had nowhere to go and slept in parks for a few weeks. One morning she stopped into a church to warm up and fell asleep in the pew. She hadn't eaten in a couple of days. About three o'clock that afternoon she was awakened by a woman who said her name was Bevie, and who told her that the church was closing and she had to leave. My mom broke down sobbing and told Bevie her story. My mom said Bevie put her arm around her and invited her home for dinner. After dinner Bevie gave her a nice warm nightgown, told her to go take a bath, and invited her to stay the night. The next morning Bevie told my mom that she and Jim wanted to offer their home to my mom until she gave birth and got on her feet. Mom and I ended up living with Aunt Bevie and Uncle Jim till I was around four years old. Aunt Bevie was the groundskeeper at the church and my mom would help her tend to the gardens.

"Aunt Bevie was always the most fun to be with. Mom and she would dance around the kitchen, entertaining me in my high chair. Uncle Jim must have watched 10,000 hours of Disney movies with me. We did crafts and planted flowers and vegetables. She taught me how to cook and sew. I realize now that she was sort of a hippie and I loved her with every fiber of my being.

"Shortly after my fourth birthday, Mom met Mike. They married six months later and we moved to Florida, where Mike was offered a great job. We were very happy until I was sixteen and they were killed in an automobile accident.

"I was heartbroken and went to stay with a cousin. I hated being at my cousin's. Their house was full of drama. Aunt Bevie called me every single day. I was depressed, acting out, failing in school, and just plain miserable. I was about to quit school. Three months later Aunt Bevie and Uncle Jim sold their house in Michigan, moved to Florida, and invited me to live with them.

"They saved my life, just as they had with my mom many years ago. Their love surrounded me and helped me heal. With Aunt Bevie I always felt safe and loved. She always encouraged me and guided me through the challenges in my life. I graduated from high school and went on to college. After college I married my high school sweetheart. A year after our wedding, my husband was transferred by his company to a job in Australia. I spoke with Aunt Bevie often but only was able to visit every couple of years.

"The year after Uncle Jim died I went to visit Aunt Bevie. She looked exhausted, she had lost a lot of weight. She kept repeating the same questions and her normally spotless house was a mess. One day she drove to the bank and did not return for hours. I was worried sick and went out looking for her. When I got back home she was there with the police. They said she almost had an accident, and when they stopped her she didn't know where she was and could not remember her address.

"It was then I realized how much Aunt Bevie needed my comfort, understanding, and help. Now it was time for me to take care of her.

"My husband and I had talked about moving back to Florida. I went home to Australia, packed my bags, and returned thee weeks later. My husband, daughter, and son-in-law sold our house and joined Aunt Bevie and me within six months. We all take care of Aunt Bevie. It is a bittersweet journey. But with love, education, support, and understanding, we are living life happily ever after."

My heart was overflowing with joy and gratitude for Mary sharing her story. She shared it with our support group the following week and continues to share her frustrations, joys, laughs, and tears on her caregiving journey.

*P.S. Mary's daughter later gave birth to a beautiful baby girl. They named her Bevie.*

*Christine Varner*

# What Are the Signs and Symptoms of Dementia — and What Should I Do?

In setting about to compose this book chapter, I thought I would be able to sit down and knock out several pages just drawing from my own personal and professional experience. My personal experience was with my beloved father. Professionally, I have worked in memory care for about fifteen years. I am a registered nurse, a licensed facility administrator, and certified teacher in Alzheimer's disease and related dementias. But instead of finding the flow and letting my knowledge and history pour forth, I found myself seeking more information and research. The "flow" was not as easily found as I anticipated.

So, as a starting point, I would like to share why this chapter is a personal journey as well as an educational piece of, I hope, helpful information. As an administrator and as the child of one who passed from dementia, I know you. I know the caregiver—the wife, the daughter, the husband, as I have, as they say, "been there and done that."

## My Daddy

I was a "daddy's girl." He was my hero, who could do anything and fix anything. His love of nature made him an expert on trees and plants. In his retirement he took up stained glass making and produced beautiful Tiffany style lamps. He was a great guy with a wicked sense of humor, a quick smile, and lots of love in his heart for his family. He was a solver of crossword puzzles and a great golfer. Oh, and he loved his brandy Old Fashioneds on the "19th" hole"!

We played golf together, with him always able to help with my stance and swing. We fished together on the many lakes of Minnesota. He helped bait my hook and haul in the "lunkers." We would sit on the patio for hours on end just chatting and cracking up over the stupidest things. It was just so much fun to be around him. Who knew what was to come?

Sixteen years ago, probably more, my father began demonstrating signs of mild memory loss that exceeded what would be considered normal for his age and health. Little things at first, then more and more evidence of progressive memory loss. We didn't know what to do, other than take him to the doctor—which he disliked mightily—in search of answers and cures.

One doctor said Daddy had something called Lewy Body disease, another said it was Alzheimer's dementia, and yet another said vascular dementia. At the time, the diagnostic tools available were pretty slim, although some simple tools are still used today. So, here we go.

*An Essential Before Testing*

A good physical exam, including a thorough basic neurological exam, should be administered before any other testing is done. Some ailments can mimic dementia and should be ruled out first, such as stroke, brain injury, Parkinson's, and others like urinary tract infection and delirium.

*Simple Testing*

In the mini-mental status exam, the doctor will ask questions like "What's the date? Who is the president? What objects are in the room?" Another simple test, called the mini-cog (for mini-cognitive), presents a list of objects and a short time later the patient is asked to repeat as many words on the list as possible. Secondly, the patient is asked to draw a clock with the numbers one to twelve drawn in order.

*More Complex Testing*

More complex testing may follow. These tests may include Computerized Tomography (CT), magnetic resonance imaging (MRI), positron emission tomography (PET), and, more recently available, molecular imaging. With molecular imaging, a compound is injected into the patient to show if Alzheimer's molecules are forming, and also show biomarkers, the genes in body fluid that may indicate the presence of the disease.

If the doctor recommends more complex testing, check with the insurance provider, as some of the more complex tests are expensive and may not be covered.

*What Are the Signs and Symptoms of Dementia?*

Almost across the expert board, the cardinal sign of dementia is memory loss, with levels categorized as mild, moderate, or severe.

Mild symptoms include:

- Trouble performing daily tasks
- Forgetting "usual" places
- Problems paying bills, handling finances
- Mild loss of judgment and bad decision-making
- Reduced action in initiative, and loss of spontaneity
- Anxiety and personality change

Moderate symptoms include:

- Increasing memory loss
- Increasing confusion

- Inability to remember friends and family members
- Decreased attention span
- Difficulties with writing, reading, and numbers
- Disorganized thinking
- Inability to handle new or unexpected situations
- Trouble learning new tasks
- Outbursts of anger and frustration
- Repetitive statements, such as telling the same story over and over again
- Paranoia
- Hallucinations
- Delusions
- Loss of "modesty" filters resulting in vulgarity, sexual acting out, undressing, etc.

Severe symptoms include:
- Loss of bladder and bowel control
- Loss of personal history (cannot recognize loved ones)
- Loss of ability to communicate, especially in communicating needs
- Weight loss
- Difficulty swallowing
- Dependence on others for completion of many, if not all, activities of daily living (bathing, grooming, dressing, feeding, etc.)
- Sleeping in excess

*What Should I Do?*

Two things need to be discussed to answer this question. First, what should I do for my loved one? Second, what should I do for myself? Each of these is of equal importance.

For your loved one:

Make sure they are getting the right medication and that it is given appropriately and on time. One "cocktail" of medication is not the answer. Often, depending on the type of dementia, a different drug or different drugs in combination are recommended.

Get into a routine: In middle stages of dementia, a common and recurring question is "what's next?" In the brain of the demented individual, there is confusion about what should follow what. Having a routine sets a calming and reassuring tone for the day. Keep it simple and keep it step-by-step—but stay just one step ahead. "Dad, we're going to go out and water the plants. Then we'll take a rest break."

Plan more-complex activities when you see your loved one is less confused and more cooperative, which is usually in the morning, than at other times. These are the times for more challenging activities. If the complex activity seems to be wearing thin, don't push.

The goal for activities in your loved one's life is to encourage as much independence as possible. It may be simpler to make the bed yourself, but allowing your loved one that independence provides a sense of accomplishment. That doesn't mean you can't help, especially if your loved one begins to develop frustration.

Keep them engaged: Rely on your knowledge of what they have engaged in before. From what did they derive pleasure? Did they play board or card games, play an instrument, listen to music, do crossword puzzles? These types of activities are not only enjoyable and relaxing, they also stimulate the brain. Stimulation helps keep the brain's nerve connections stronger, and more blood flowing to the brain for nourishment.

Exercise: Again, knowing what types of exercise were stimulating in the past is a key component in planning exercise on a daily basis. Tennis, golf, shuffleboard, jogging? If physical skills are not as sharp as they once were, simply walking is great.

Other engagement: Watching television is not recommended as a mentally engaging pastime. Nonetheless, some TV is calming, reassuring, and entertaining. Tried-and-true programs such as Jeopardy, The Price Is Right, and Wheel of Fortune are programs many older adults have watched for years. There is a familiarity to these shows that brings contentment and stimulates participation.

And let's not forget televised sports. For both many a male and female, the Saturday or Sunday ritual of watching a favorite team is part of our culture. I have known many people with cognitive impairment who still enjoy rooting for their team, wearing their team colors, and decorating their rooms with posters and memorabilia.

Pets may or may not be a part of a person's past. Again, your knowledge of your loved one's likes and dislikes can bring pure pleasure into the household by keeping a pet or having pets visit. A pet owned by your loved one can give him or her a sense of purpose as well—feeding, walking, and grooming Fluffy is therapeutic and stimulating.

A good diet: Try to stick to a heart- and brain-healthy diet. These foods include fruits, nuts, vegetables, and a few surprises.

- Nuts and seeds—are important sources of vitamin E and omega-3 fatty acids.
- Beets—contain nitrates, which increase blood flow to brain.
- Oats—provide glucose to "feed" the brain.
- Lean meats—provide vitamins and iron.
- Flax seed—is a great source of alpha-Linolenic acid, which reduces stress and increases performance.
- Lentils (red, green, orange, black)—are a source of

folate (Vitamin B9).

- Dark chocolate—includes antioxidants.
- Berries and cherries—blueberries are so important they're now dubbed "brainberries."
- Vegetable juice—is a source of vitamin B12.
- Avocados—like blueberries, they have "brainberry" properties.
- Salmon—is high in omega 3 fatty acids and anti-inflammatories.
- Spinach, kale, broccoli—and all leafy green vegetables are an important source of beneficial nutrients and antioxidants.
- Onions—help improve immunity and reduce inflammation.

There are lists and lists of these brain-enhancing foods, but caution must be used as some of the claims are not proven. Also, some supplements are not FDA-approved for this use, and only make money off desperate or uniformed people. Be sure to consult reliable sources such as FDA lists, the Mayo Clinic, and the Alzheimer's Association for more guidance.

Of course there are some favorites that are just not to be done without! Ice cream, anyone?

Music: I don't think I have cared for a single person with dementia who did not relate, in some way, to music. Music—and singing—connects them to past times and events that are meaningful, and often bring about wonderful memories. Through your and your loved one's lifetimes, certain types of music, musicians, and songs come to have special meaning that can help engage them. For whatever reason, music stays with a person long after they may have forgotten other activities or skills. It is speculated that the auditory system is the first to develop and thus the last to leave.

It will help if you can develop a "playlist" of favorites. Play these songs on CDs and sing along. The playlist can be recorded or saved to an iPod or mp3 device. Using headphones (but not earbuds) allows your loved one to listen and sing along to their favorites. Or use your computer or tablet to find and stream music from radio broadcasts of long ago. (Old Radio World offers a lot to choose from.) After listening to the music, take a few moments to talk about certain songs and help your loved one reminisce about where they were when they first heard those songs, and what they were doing.

Music is often a very useful adjunct to making the completion of activities of daily life simpler. For example, often a person with dementia becomes resistant to bathing or showering. Putting on favorite, relaxing music during this process may make a sometimes difficult process easier.

*Communication Dos and Don'ts*

Imagine yourself in a room with loud music, multiple conversations going on, a TV blaring, and lot of movement happening around you while you are trying to concentrate on writing a letter. It's difficult to focus when being bombarded by all that! In the brain of someone with dementia, sensory overload can occur with much less stimulation and may stand in the way of engaging in meaningful communication.

Reducing distraction is a first step in communicating effectively. Create a quiet and comfortable area in the house. Turn off the television. Make eye contact and use your loved one's name frequently: "John, let's talk about the wonderful times we danced at the USO. You were the best dancer in the room, John."

When it is clear your loved one is having trouble recognizing you or family members, don't play guessing games—this is not the time for Twenty Questions! Identify yourself rather than waiting to be recognized or asking "Do you know who I am?" Say, "Hi Dad, it's your daughter Chrissy. I'm so glad to see you today." There is absolutely no reason to challenge your loved one's recall of significant persons in their life. Tell your friends, children, neighbors, and others to introduce themselves and say how they are connected to your loved one. Often, this can kick-start a meaningful visit. At times, it may be useful to wear a name tag—Chrissy, Your Daughter—or even use a picture of yourself taken at a time that still is readily remembered.

Your loved one is an adult who happens to have a progressive memory disorder. While you should speak slowly and clearly, avoid speaking as if your loved one is a child. You may need to use simple words and short sentences but always do so in a way that preserves your loved one's dignity.

Be patient! The disease that is affecting your loved one's brain has messed up the actual physiology of their brain. Once-normal proteins in the brain are breaking down, leaving byproducts like tangles (from dead and dying nerve cells) and plaques. This slows the ability of your loved one to process information. So, patience is a virtue. Allow them to "digest" what you are talking about. Try not to hurry this process along by dropping hints or clues. Your reward will be consistent and more meaningful communication.

*Difficult Behavior*

No matter how smoothly life may proceed, there will be times when ugly dementia behaviors rear their heads. Commonly, these are manifested in actions or speech that are aggressive in nature and stem from fear, frustration or even physical discomfort that is either not verbalized or cannot be. Be sure to check for causes that can be easily eliminated or changed, which are usually environmental in nature. Trying to drill down on the cause of the behavior can be difficult, but it will be rewarding when the cause of the behavior is identified and can be ameliorated.

Remember that all behaviors have meaning. The aggressive or acting out behaviors are not intentional—they are part of the disease process.

*Medications*

In most cases, your doctor will prescribe your loved one such medications as Aricept®, Exelon®, and Namenda. These are most often treatment for the dementia itself. The medications may act in different ways but all are intended to slow the disease process. At times, medications may also be prescribed for depression and mood swings.

In all cases, make sure your doctor is willing and able to describe the actions of the medications, when and how they should be administered, and all possible side effects. And remember that, while still able, it may be satisfying for your loved one to have some control over managing the medication regimen.

Aricept, Exelon, and Namenda are typically prescribed for Alzheimer's disease. Other dementias may require different medications. It's important to know that use of the standard Alzheimer's meds may, in fact, have a reverse or adverse effect on people who suffer from a different form of dementia.

*For You, the Caregiver*

Those of us who caregive have a tough row to hoe. As much as we all think of ourselves as the super-caretaker of the year, there is a limit to what we can handle, physically and emotionally. The stories you may hear of caregivers pre-deceasing their loved ones are true.

What you cannot control is the disease process. What you can control is how you manage your feelings and responses.

Most commonly, the stressed caregiver's feelings are based in frustration. The constant requirement to be the 24/7 caregiver is fraught with situations that frustrate you, and affect your mood and ability to respond in a caring and effective way.

This requires that you take a moment from time to time to take your "emotional pulse." If possible, take a few minutes to get away. Count to ten. Take deep breaths. Take a walk. Go to church. Visit neighbors. If you have friends who understand your circumstances, reach out to them to see if they can pitch hit for you for a brief time.

Anger, frustration, depression—the whole gamut of feelings, may begin to envelope you and can, quite literally, make you sick. You may experience headaches, knots in your throat and stomach, chest pain, and shortness of breath. If you drink alcohol or smoke, you may notice an increase in use. All of these reactions can be mitigated, if not eliminated, when you are able to stop for a moment and recognize your escalating negative feelings.

Look for ways you can develop a set of relaxation techniques to initiate as soon as you identify mounting frustration. Just as with any other habit, these techniques can become rote. Get away for a moment, deep breathe, meditate, take a walk, take a bath. Whatever works for you is what works for you!

### Don't Be Afraid to Ask

Sometimes we get caught up in our own little world of duties and responsibilities. We believe we are the only one who can fulfill the role of caregiver to our loved one. We think we are the only one who knows what to do when, what medications are needed when, how to occupy our loved one's time, how to keep them engaged and stimulated.

Well, you are not the Lone Ranger. There are many, many other caregivers out there who are caught in this same trap of feeling "I am the only one."

Be willing to say yes to offers of help, and at the same time be ready to say "no" to family members, organizations, or friends who make demands that you cannot meet.

Now is the time to realize that you not only can, but must ask for help! One of the best resources is the Alzheimer's Association. Visit the website or call them at 1-800-272-3900, as they have resources you may not even have considered and listings that will direct you to a host of support groups in your area.

Also check around or inquire with the association for local adult day-stay centers, communities that offer respite stays, or at-home assistance with a companion or nursing assistant.

You need, and deserve, time for yourself. Your burnout and frustration factors, as well as your own health, are concerns you cannot and should not ignore.

Remember to eat well, get out of the house, sleep well, and monitor your sense of well-being. See your doctor. Make sure that he or she understands the situation that you are in. Sometimes you may need medication too, to fight off possible depression.

*Family Time*

A discussion with your family is something you should have now, long before you reach your limit as a caregiver. While many family members will be empathetic and ready to step up to the challenge of helping, some may "pooh-pooh" the tremendous stress and frustration you carry. Ask family members who are not willing to see your side to come for a day, a few days or even a week, to care for your loved one while you get away. Not surprisingly, it may only take a few hours for them to throw up their hands and ask, "How do you do this every day?"

The family discussion must include planning for the future. When and for how long will long-term care become necessary? What resources do you have as an individual and collectively as a family for making such a decision? Who and when should you consult legal and financial planning? A Power of Attorney, Healthcare Surrogate, and Living Will are imperative and powerful documents that you should have in place for your loved one. In some states, a state form must be completed and signed by a physician in order to put a "Do Not Resuscitate Order" (DNR) or "Physician Orders for Life Sustaining Treatment" (POLST) in place.

Millions of people across the world are diagnosed with dementia. It is a progressive disease that will not get better. Your single responsibility is to get smart and stay smart about the disease, the role you play in caregiving, the toll it can take on you, and the resources available to you when you need them.

Resources
There are many books and articles that provide important information. Here are some others recommended by the Alzheimer's Association and the National Institute on Aging.

The 36-hour Day: A Family Guide to Caring for People With Alzheimer's Disease, Other Dementias, and Memory Loss in Later Life: http://amzn.to/1T8LioC

Mayo Clinic Guide to Alzheimer's Disease: The Essential Resource for Treatment, Coping and Caregiving: http://amzn.to/1LoO2Lk

The Alzheimer's Action Plan: The Experts' Guide to the Best Diagnosis and Treatment for Memory Problems

Alzheimer's Early Stages: First Steps for Family, Friends and Caregivers: http://amzn.to/1NqzYCd
The Forgetting: Alzheimer's: Portrait of an Epidemic: http://amzn.to/1XliUzz

Other Resources
Old Radio World: http://bit.ly/1U4FOv5

*Christine Varner has been an executive director in memory care for more than fifteen years. A Registered Nurse with additional education in healthcare administration, she is certified in assisted living core training and extended congregate care. Additionally, Christine is recognized by the State of Florida as an Alzheimer's Trainer for state-mandated Alzheimer's trainings, and is author of numerous articles on Alzheimer's and related dementias.*

## Purple Cities Alliance

The Purple Cities Alliance is a global network dedicated to creating dementia-friendly communities by educating first-responders, health care providers, public-service providers, retailers, and the public about the needs of people struggling with dementia. The purpose is to create communities that act consciously to ensure that people with dementia are respected, empowered, engaged, and embraced, so they may live as independent and enjoyable a life as possible in safety and dignity.

People who provide universal and non-specialist services and activities that people with dementia have used in the past (and will want to continue to use) find that awareness training for their staff increases their understanding of people's needs. That awareness has the potential to improve the customer experience, ensuring the continued patronage of the person with dementia and their caregiver, and it allows staff to feel they are doing a better job of meeting their customers' needs.

To learn more, visit the Purple City Campaign, and follow the Purple Cities Alliance on Facebook.

*Linda Burhans*

## A Blast from the Past

I had done some one-on-one coaching with Mike and he also attended a number of my support groups.

Recently his wife, who had dementia, had come to the point where she was unable to remember him. She would tell him, "I don't know who you are. You're not my husband."

Mike talked at the support groups about how difficult this was for him. They had been married more than fifty years and, he said, she was the only gal for him.

Not long ago Mike called me. "I have some wonderful news, Linda. I was lying in bed the other night and could not sleep. I kept remembering how you said I need to go into my wife's world, because she cannot come into mine. And then suddenly it came to me.

"The next morning I went to my hair salon and had them dye my white hair back to black, and cut it in the same style I wore when we were first dating. Then I went out and bought myself a pair blue jeans and a white T-shirt. At home I found the surfer's cross she gave me when we were twenty years old. I got dressed and went to visit her. When I walked in I called her the pet name I had for her when we were younger. And guess what, Linda? I'm her new boyfriend!"

I broke out in goosebumps. Mike's love for his wife was

so strong that he took a big risk. I am absolutely delighted that it worked out for him. Thinking creatively might work for you, too!

*Carole Ware-McKenzie*

## How Can I Be Engaged with My Loved One?

When I walked into the building, I saw many people sitting in chairs. There was a combination of wheel chairs, Gerri chairs, and everyday chairs. The people didn't look unhappy, uncomfortable, or in any danger—they were just simply sitting in the chairs. I made eye contact with one beautiful lady with shiny, silver hair that was brushed straight back. I smiled and said, "Good morning. How are you today?" I saw something change in her and she seemed to light up. When I stepped closer and bent down to her eye level, touched her hand, and told her I loved her hair, she immediately responded to my touch and to my words with a grin that seemed to actually make the room a little brighter. "Thank you," she said and she stroked her hair. Then, like so many women uncomfortable accepting a compliment, she said, "I need to go the beauty shop." I told her I thought it looked lovely the way it is. "But I do understand that we women always feel a little better after we have been to the beauty shop!" We both giggled a little and exchanged names and a few niceties. She told me to have a wonderful day and I said, "You too. It was nice to meet you."

The whole interaction took no longer than three or four minutes but it impacted me. I realized that no matter the advancements in healthcare or all our modern technologies, regardless of our age we all desire and need the chance for true engagement. We, as human beings, need to be seen and heard, to confirm that we are still here. In today's world we can connect with anyone in a matter of seconds halfway around the world, yet sometimes we can be in the same room and not have a meaningful interaction.

As care partners we often become overwhelmed with the tasks of the day—cooking meals, doing laundry, going to the doctor, grocery shopping, and the hundred-and-one things that need to be done. We are often so focused on taking care of our loved one that we forget to be with our loved one. Sometimes, it is the one thing that we can control in a caregiving situation. Yes, we can control the list of to-dos, and we can get the satisfaction of marking off at least a few of the items on that endless list. We cannot fix our loved one's struggle in trying to move from the kitchen to the living room but we can fix dinner. But, if we are not careful, we might just miss the blessing of being involved with the one we're caring for.

When we are responsible for another human being, whether it is a family member–or someone we are working with in a professional capacity, we have to be conscious of the impact we can have. The more we can find ways to engage, the more the relationship can be strengthened, which in turn can assist in many different areas affecting elders.

Using engagement is a very effective tool in decreasing negative behaviors, especially in with those living with dementia. More and more research is being done that shows the benefits and desirable effects that positive socialization, wellness programs, and engagement programs have on our elders. Here are just some of those benefits:

- Potentially reduced risk for cardiovascular problems, some cancers, osteoporosis, and rheumatoid arthritis
- Potentially improved immune system
- Potentially reduced risk for Alzheimer's disease
- Improved memory

- Lowered blood pressure
- Reduced risk for mental health issues, such as depression and personality disorders
- Reduced stress and improved quality of sleep
- Increased length of time of independence

The impacts of social isolation have been proven to have many negative impacts on our elders. For those who enjoy the good read of a comprehensive scholarly article, check out "A Review of Social Isolation," by Nicholas R. Nicholson in The Journal of Primary Prevention. Its introduction observes bluntly that, "social isolation has been demonstrated to lead to numerous detrimental health effects in older adults, including increased risk health complications, dementia, increased risk for re-hospitalization, and an increased number of falls." It is one of those things that made good common sense to us before, and now we have the research backing up what we knew to be true.

So what are we really talking about when we say engagement? The Webster Dictionary's definition of engagement is "a promise to meet or be present at a particular place and time." If we focus on the being part of the definition, we can take our everyday activities and turn them into engagement opportunities. Areas we can concentrate on for the purpose of engaging elders can be found in the categories that follow. Though a few examples are given in each category, don't be limited by them. You could start your journey of excitement and engagement with an elder by having a discussion and determining what your individual care partner team believes is important in each of the categories.

- Emotional—peer counseling, stress management, humor/laughter, and remembrance
- Intellectual—journaling, arts and crafts, cognitive

games and puzzles

- Physical—exercise and movement, nutrition, sleep, disease management
- Social—clubs or group activities
- Spiritual—faith-based, personal meditation/reflection, mindful exercise
- Vocational—volunteer work, skills classes
- Artistic—music, poetry, painting, theater

How can you engage a loved one who seems to spend more and more time in front of the TV and is less and less interested in activities they used to enjoy? This is where creativity and engagement can really flourish. Often I have noted that as elders become more sedentary and less interested in the activities they once enjoyed, they will mask their fear and anxiety about trying things behind an attitude of non-interest. Sometimes they may even respond in anger and lash out. If the care partners weather the storm by taking time and finding the energy to try different methods, they might find a way to break through.

Here's an example. Paul, who was seventy-six, used to play golf at least three times a week. He had loved going to the clubhouse and talking with his many friends as much as getting out on the course. He loved the game, whether talking about it, watching it on TV, reading magazines, or competing against his friends and boasting he could have gone pro if he hadn't gone into the military. But at the age of seventy-five, Paul had a stroke that impacted his speech slightly and he was having more and more issues with his memory. He was not quite as steady on his feet as he once was, and used a cane when he was outside of his house. After his stroke, he seemed to lose interest in anything to do with golf.

After a few conversations with Paul, his family realized he

had not lost interest in golf but instead didn't think he could enjoy it any longer. A plan was put together to slowly try to re-introduce Paul to his passion of the game. Though it was somewhat overwhelming for him at first, a discussion helped explore what some of his fears were. Some ideas of how to engage him came from a team meeting that consisted of his wife, his out-of-state son, his twelve-year-old grandson (who already loved the game), and a private duty health care worker who had never even been on a golf course. The team, including Paul, knew that the plan would have to move slowly, that they couldn't just jump in and expect him to feel comfortable.

Paul and his son started by talking about some of the tournaments that were coming up on television. They agreed to "meet" on Skype while watching one. His home health aide found some golf books and pictures and started asking questions of Paul, to understand the basics of the game and why he found it so enjoyable. Since the home health aide had no knowledge of the game, Paul was in the role of "instructor" and felt he had something to offer. Eventually they got out his home putting equipment and had a few laughs as the home health aide tried to make a few shots, again under Paul's tutelage. Paul's wife reminisced with him about some of the foursomes they'd played over the years with friends. Paul's grandson told stories his coaches were sharing with him, then got his grandfather's perspective and advice as well. Soon Paul was finding new ways to enjoy the game he loved for so long. The family planned a golf excursion and Paul joined them, riding in the cart, enjoying watching the others play, and sharing his years of wisdom. He no longer could play a round of 18 holes, but he was able to still get enjoyment from the game because others took the time to engage him. They were truly present with him while he learned to reconnect with his love of golf in a new manner.

As you can imagine, it sounds much easier than it actually is. Paul did not wake up one morning to find that the plan was in place and that the care partner team was 100 percent engaged. It takes time and patience to build or strengthen relationships in a way that fosters true engagement.

Here are a few tips I have found helpful in doing so. Some of these will work with a loved one and some will not. I believe that engagement is the ultimate game of trial and error. Try some of these techniques and see where it leads you. If it works, continue doing it and if it doesn't, try something else. There is no perfect formula so if you just make a commitment to try, I guarantee you will experience some measure of success.

*Question Everything*

A great way to learn about someone new or even someone you have known for years is by asking questions that can't be answered by yes or no. Depending on abilities and limitations, it will be different for each person. Overall, if you know someone has a special interest in something, such as jazz music, start by asking a simple question and see where that leads you. When there is the opportunity for someone to share something with you, the opportunity will then be there for you to ask questions, and to have a good chance that they might share their thoughts. That is engagement! I always say there is a reason God gave us two ears and one mouth.

Be observant of verbal and non-verbal cues—Even if your loved one cannot communicate verbally, they surely will let you know how they are feeling. Make sure you are not trying to multi-task every time you are with them. Sometimes you have to slow down and sit down with them, face to face, to really hear what they are saying. Pay attention to what seems to make their eyes sparkle.

Look for clues, play the detective—If you do not know

a lot about their previous life (before they needed your extra assistance), see what type of books, music, and things they have around their house. Use those clues to ask questions, in order to find out more about who they are. Just realize, when you are looking at that lady in her wheelchair, that is not the sum of who she is. She had dreams, goals, and adventures that are still playing in her head. Recognize that your short-tempered father-in-law, who seems to never be satisfied, was once a young boy who loved playing practical jokes on his siblings. Do what you can to revive that young lad who loved to laugh over the Abbott and Costello radio show. Be the detective; don't assume that all you see is all there is.

*Think Out of the Box*

Try something new. At one point there was the belief that individuals with dementia needed a very structured routine and that you didn't want to try anything new. To be sure, routine and structure help to assist in preparing for the day. But you can mix it up a little bit. If the norm is to eat breakfast and look over the paper, try pulling up some famous headlines of the day from different years and have a discussion on how things are different from the 1940s to the 1980s to today. If the routine is a walk around the block in the afternoon, suggest going to the park for the walk. Or pull out some art supplies. I have seen many amazing art pieces done by individuals who did not start painting until they were in their seventies or eighties, and some didn't start until after the diagnosis of Alzheimer's.

*Don't Treat Them as a Child, But Don't Be Afraid to Have Fun*

If we think about it, some of our fondest memories come from when we are with our friends and just being silly. You never want to talk down to someone or make them feel "less than." But sometimes putting on some music and doing the

Hokey Pokey cannot only be a stress reliever, it can be a great way to get in a little exercise without even realizing it. I always refer back to myself, where one of the most relaxing things for me is to color. Some professionals used to squawk at the idea of our elders coloring. I don't advocate getting a child's coloring book and box of crayons and telling everyone to go to town. It has recently became quite the trend, now you can find many adult coloring books. Coloring mandalas is always a fun choice, and they can even try their hand at Tangle Art, which is fancy doodling. Pastels or colored pencils are a great alternative to crayons.

George Bernard Shaw said a mouthful when he said, "We don't stop playing because we grow old; we grow old because we stop playing."
Use music, and more music—I always like playing background music at low volume while doing activities. In fact, I could write a whole chapter on the power of music. Research shows that by simply adding music to an activity, the elders tend to view the activity more favorably, and this is especially so with movement and exercise. Music is a great way to liven up a range-of-motion exercise. Make sure you use the type of music they enjoy. We are soon approaching the days where we will walk into an elder exercise class with the Rolling Stones playing instead of Dean Martin. If you'd like more information on the power of music, an excellent article is Music and Memory: Elders with Dementia Find Hope in a Song, in the Jan-Feb 2013 issue of Social Work Today.

*Get Up Close and Personal*

Make sure, when you are trying to connect, that you are doing it up close and personally. When speaking to someone, make sure you are at eye level, but are not hovering over them. This is where dignity comes into play. If I had someone standing above me and demanding it was time to take a shower and get cleaned up, I imagine I would turn a little feisty too. Sit down near them and look them in the eyes, perhaps give them a slight touch on their hand. Let them have a say in moving from one activity to the next. It is important to prepare them by giving verbal cues about moving on to the next item on the schedule. Make it a gentle reminder, out of courtesy, and not because they are always forgetting (even if they are). For example, you might say, "Mom, after breakfast I thought I would work on the scrapbook. Would you like to help?" You can give choices by posing a question, such as, "What are you in the mood for today after breakfast? Would you like to go for a walk or do the chair exercises?"

*Process vs. Product*

This is my favorite saying when it comes to activity and engagement. Process is important in every task our loved ones do. Sure, it is easier to put her shoes on for her and to tie them for her, but sometimes we need to slow down and allow them the time to complete the task. I have learned that if I am not patient enough to wait for answers and I think that someone is not going to respond, I may possibly miss some great one-liners. The end product is not nearly as important as the process of getting to the end.

This was best demonstrated when I was doing a craft with a group and one of the volunteers was trying so hard to make sure her participant's craft looked exactly like the example. She completely took over. The participant sat quietly and smiled as the volunteer finished. It looked nice, but the participant got nothing from the activity because she was merely an observer. This is a common error, and a grave one. It is better to allow the participants the time and opportunity to do the tasks. Yes, it will take much longer and it might not look like what was intended, but it is well worth it when they have the satisfaction of knowing that they completed it.

If the individual has dementia, he might not even recall that he just completed the task, but he still can experience that feeling of value during the time of actually doing the work. I love doing art projects because they always bring a discussion where everyone views art differently. There is always some redeeming quality about an art piece, even if it is the laughter of getting glitter everywhere and sparkling for the rest of day.

Make sure to find an activity you both enjoy. If you hate cooking it might not be a good idea to try to engage your loved one in the kitchen. You should truly enjoy it yourself in order to get someone else excited about doing it. But you can try to find an aspect of the activity that you do enjoy, such as looking at cookbooks and finding interesting recipes, which allows you to engage. That is why talking to the entire care team is important; each person brings unique interests and talents to the table.

Be silly, have fun, and laugh a whole lot—I start each of my groups or activities by saying what we are going to be doing. Whether it is poetry, movement or art, I always state that the main goal is to giggle and laugh, because everyone always needs a good giggle. I know this has been my lifesaver when an activity did not turn out to be as amazing as I thought it would be. Instead, the fun and engagement becomes centered on how bad an idea it is!

Have fun and take the opportunity to be with another human. We are human beings. Sometimes we just forget to be. When we learn to be truly present with another, engagement happens.

Resources:

LinkedSenior: 6 Health Benefits of Having Hobbies
     & Leisure Activities: http://bit.ly/1LE1gCp

Music & Memory: www.musicandmemory.org

National Center for Creative Aging: www.creativeaging.org

Virginia Bell and Davie Troxel's Best Friends™ Approach to
     Alzheimer's Care: http://amzn.to/1TQp8EF

Memory Bridge: www.memorybridge.org

National Council on Aging: www.ncoa.org

Good Old Days, the Magazine that Remembers the Best:
     www.goodolddaysmagazine.com

Reminisce magazine: www.reminisce.com

RadioLovers Old Time Radio Shows:
     www.radiolovers.com

*Carole Ware-McKenzie has used her skills and talents to engage
others for more than twenty-five years. She has spent the last twelve
years working with elders. She created H.E.A.R.T.S (Healing
trough Expressive Arts and Recreational Therapy Services), a unique
engagement program. She loves working families and professional
care partners to break through those perceived barriers to enhance and
strengthen communication and relationship. She has a B.S. degree
in Recreation and Psychology and is trained in many different
modalities of experiential therapies and expressive arts. For more
information contact Carole@touchinghearts1by1.com or on Facebook.*

*Linda Burhans*

## Queen of the House

Paul had been coming to one of my caregivers' support groups for a while. His wife had early onset dementia and lived in a wonderful memory community.

One day after a support group, he asked if he could meet with me alone. "My wife is failing and it's breaking my heart," he said. "In fact, she even has a boyfriend who also lives in the community. Many times when I go to visit her, she's sitting next to him and holding his hand. Sometimes I just sit on the other side and hold her other hand.

"I get it," he said. "I know she doesn't really know who I am anymore. But I just miss my girl. The one time she does seem to make connection with me, though, is twice a month when the guitar player comes and plays music for all the residents."

After a moment he asked, "Linda, did you ever hear that song 'King of the Road'?"

"Sure," I replied. Roger Miller's song had been a huge hit in 1965. In my mind I could immediately hear, "...trailers for sale or rent, rooms to let, fifty cents..."

Paul then took my hand and told me a little story. When that song was all over the airwaves, his wife wrote a song that was a take-off on "King of the Road." She titled it "Queen of the House."

"We were young and we didn't think to copyright it. We sent the song to Nashville. Another singer picked it up and claimed credit. I was angry for a long time, but if I could just hear that song again, it would warm my heart. It's all about our family."

Paul's words planted an idea in my head. I decided to see if I could find a copy of her song. It took me a few weeks of searching but finally I did. A few days later the perfect 45 rpm record arrived in the mail.

I took the record to the director of the community where Paul's wife lived. She said she would have it made into a CD by a friend of hers and the planning began. I contacted Paul's children and said I wanted their help to create a surprise for their dad. I asked them for photos of their parents taken around the time their mom wrote the song.

A couple weeks later we all made plans to be at their mother's community on the day the guitar player came. I took the CD of Paul's wife's song on a portable boom-box. And we also made sure her "boyfriend" was away on a field trip that day.

The guitarist played for about an hour and everyone was having a good time. Paul's wife sat next to him quietly, with her head down.

"Any requests?" the guitarist asked.

"How about 'King of the Road'?" our plant called out.

The guitarist performed the song and then asked if there were any other requests.

Now, this was God speaking if you ask me—Paul muttered, "Yeah. I'd love to hear 'Queen of the House.'"

Immediately the guitarist turned on the song. Paul

was astonished. Then his wife slowly raised her head. Her children were calling out, "Mom, that's your song!" Paul stood up and took his wife's hand. She rose, and the two of them danced to the entire song.

Later, we presented Paul a shadowbox we had put together—in it was a copy of the original record and family photos.

Paul turned to me with tears in his eyes. "Thank you so much. Please, I want you to meet my wife."

I sat down next to her and took her hand. She spoke a little bit, but nothing she said made much sense. Suddenly she stopped. She looked into my eyes and said, "Thank you. I love you."

My heart was overjoyed, and there wasn't a dry eye in the room.

One of the best things that resulted from that day is, the community now celebrates the life of a different resident every few weeks. One woman used to be the "donut queen" of her town. On "her" day, she was allowed to go into the kitchen with her family and the staff and make donuts for all the residents. Another resident had been an expert golfer. They set up an area where he could golf and also teach the other residents.

Yes, everyone has a story, and a past. Maybe as William Faulkner said, "The past is never dead. It's not even past."

*If you'd like to hear "Queen of the House," it's on YouTube.*

*Rebecca Weitzel*

# Is a Memory Care Community the Right Choice for My Loved One?

Have you ever made a promise to someone? I imagine you can recall different times and circumstances in life where you made a promise to someone you loved. This is our nature; this is one way that we show each other that we care—deeply. When making a promise, I think most people are sincere in the pact they are entering into and truly intend to carry out their end of the bargain. But let's face it, promises are made, circumstances change, and then we feel guilty for not coming through. Over the course of my career in assisting families through the heartbreak of Alzheimer's and related dementias, one of the emotions that often surfaces is guilt. Guilt about breaking a promise made in years past, a promise that was well intentioned but a promise made without the benefit of knowing what the future would hold.

Ten, twenty, thirty years ago, we didn't hear such things as "early onset," Lewy Body dementia, familial Alzheimer's, frontotemporal, mild cognitive impairment, and dementia. The closest we got back then was the rare whisperings of senility—memory loss was something that occasionally happened to old people and, when it was recognized, folks tended to write it off as a rare occurrence, something to be pitied, but certainly not something that would likely happen to them or their loved ones. Today we know that dementia touches the lives of many families. If you are fortunate enough to not be among this group, chances are that you know someone who has not been so lucky. The World Health Organization reports that there are 47.5 million people worldwide with dementia and this number is growing by 7.7 million new diagnoses each year.

As we are recognizing what the prevalence of this statistic means, we are becoming more educated and aware of its presence in those we care for and love. Looking back decades ago, without the knowledge we have today, it's easy to see how spouses, children, and friends made promises that, no matter what, "I will never put you away in one of those old folks' homes. I, myself, will take care of you always." When making such a promise, what was not known was there could come a day when they might not be able to care for their loved one in all ways.

Daily, I work with families struggling with the decision to place a loved one in a care community because of such promises made years past. The very fact that they made a promise and cannot keep it brings out feelings of guilt, anxiousness, and broken trust. There is never anyone or any place that can take care of our loved ones as well as we can, but it's important to understand that often there comes a time when the individual spouse or child is not equipped to provide the best care. The Alzheimer's Association's research documents that caregivers are often at risk for serious illness and death, brought on by the stresses of providing care, and frequently die before those they are caring for.

A question worthy of asking is: "If Mom knew, twenty-five years ago, that she was going to have dementia, that it was a progressive disease, and that I was going to be the only one around to care for her, that providing this care could put me at risk of illness and even death before her, would she ask or expect me to make such a promise?"

I recently heard a speaker talk about the guilt associated

with no longer being able to care for a loved one with dementia. She noted that the feelings accompanying diseases that cause dementia are not commonly associated with other types of fatal illnesses. As an example, consider someone suffering through terminal cancer. The loved ones provide care for as long as they feel they can best meet the needs of their loved one, but are quick to understand their own limitations and to recognize when their loved one's needs are beyond their capacity. This is often the time that the cancer patient is placed into the care of others, such as a hospital or hospice facility.

Because the caregiver is accepting of the fact that the needs of their loved one can better be tended to in an environment equipped for such care, and carried out by professionals trained specifically to tend to the needs of these patients, the decision to make such a transition is not accompanied by the negative feelings accompanying the dementia caregiver. Why is this so? Why do caregivers of dementia patients have more difficulty recognizing and admitting when the time has come for professional help, in a setting designed and equipped specifically for the optimum care their loved one needs?

One reason may be simply that we can see the effects of cancer, while the ravaging effects of dementia remain invisible. When our loved one looks sick and frail, it seems we can more easily acknowledge our caregiving limitations and look for help in other places. Because dementia is not easily seen by looking at someone, it's almost as if our brain is telling us that this person isn't really sick. This person isn't dying, they seem fine—other than their memory loss, they look and act perfectly normal. For this reason my mission has been to help families recognize this paradox and, in doing so, to be able to let go of the guilt they are carrying and make the best decision they can with the information they have today, not from the position they were in years past.

Shifting focus into a realistic approach does not make the decision any less unpleasant, but it can remove the angst, guilt, and unrealistic expectations in which caregivers become trapped. The dementia journey is fraught with difficultly. As a society we can help by removing the stigma associated with seeking care in an assisted living community. Remove the notion that we are "putting them away," that we don't care enough. Rather, we need to realize that we know there are times when the help of others is what is needed to give our loved ones the best care for their current circumstances, and that by giving them the care they deserve we are showing that we do care enough.

There is no heroism in going it alone. Imagine the quality of life improving for both you and your loved one as they transition from their home into a community designed to provide the optimum environment for their needs in living with dementia. I have witnessed a remarkable transition take place for families in crisis as I've seen wives, husbands, and children discover renewed strength when their stress is lessened and their sleepless nights eliminated. When this happens, the time spent with their loved one shifts from a task of labor and hardship back to a shared time of quality and enjoyment unencumbered by the need to be a sole provider of care.

I believe that when old promises are revisited using the knowledge and wisdom we have today, what we really mean to say is, "I promise to take care of you the best way that I can, and I will continue to love you always and in all ways."

*Making the Transition*
When a family determines that the time to seek outside care for their loved one has come, it is important to understand the different options available and to choose the one most appropriate for their needs. A good place to start researching

care options is home health. Home health companies provide care to people in their own homes. These services can be used from a few hours a day up to around-the-clock care. This option can give the primary caregiver relief that ranges from a break to allowing them to continue working full-time, while providing peace of mind that their loved one is safe and being cared for while they are away.

There are circumstances which may require care be provided outside of the person's home. When this is the case, an assisted living community may present a good option. When considering assisted living for someone with dementia, it is important to select a community that specializes in care for the memory-impaired. Taking care of someone with dementia requires a different skill set than does taking care of someone with a healthy brain. Care partners working in communities designed for those with Alzheimer's and related dementias have specialized training and use a different approach than do caregivers assisting people who have healthy brains. When doing your research, seek communities that provide specialized memory care, and talk with both management and staff about their approach and how their care is delivered.

As I speak to people needing care, I find it is not uncommon for them to refer to assisted living as a nursing home. It is important to recognize the difference between these two types of facilities. Assisted living is designed to provide care for people in a home-like setting, where residents continue to go about their lives and, as much as possible, can participate in the everyday tasks, chores, and hobbies they have always enjoyed. In contrast, nursing homes are designed to provide care using a medical model, similar to a hospital setting. Nursing homes historically are institutions that provide care for those with highly acute physical needs. While some people with dementia may require 24/7 nursing care in a skilled facility as their dementia progresses, it is often not the case during the time that families are looking to transition care away from home into an outside community.

The best way to understand the differences between an assisted living community and a nursing home is to visit both types of facilities. When families do this, the differences between the two environments are readily identified and understood. Also, during these visits, families are often able to determine which level of care is most appropriate for the current needs of their loved one.

*Choosing the Right Community for Your Loved One*
If the decision to seek care in an assisted living community is deemed appropriate, the likely next step will be to tour different places. When visiting communities, do your best to look past the façade and focus on the actual care being delivered to residents. Just because an assisted living community is pretty doesn't necessarily mean it will be the best selection for your loved one.

Once you have narrowed your choice to a few communities, it is wise to visit them more than once and at different times of the day—and also to go at night. I recommend dropping in without an appointment, and spending time observing the environment and what is happening during your stay. Talk with other resident families and the care staff. Talk to people in the nursing and administrative departments to get a feel for their philosophy of care and values. Considering a short stay for your loved one before making a long-term commitment may be a good way to learn more about a specific community and the care they provide. This can be done by utilizing day-stays, short-term, and respite stays the community may offer. One of the most important outcomes of this decision is for the family members and caregivers to have peace of mind and to feel confident their loved one is in the place that is just right.

(Note: For some memory-impaired individuals, this may not be a viable option as it may be too disruptive and unsettling to temporarily and repeatedly change an environment and social setting. All circumstances are different. Talk with a professional and seek advice while considering your options.)

*Finding Help*

It is not uncommon for families to find themselves thrust into crisis situations for which they are not prepared. Because dementia is invisible to the naked eye, it is easy to hide or cover up the disease that is causing the symptoms, especially from family members and friends who are living away from the person with memory impairment. Furthermore, a spouse may help disguise an illness out of denial or due to fear and lack of knowledge, in order to protect others from what they are experiencing. The child of an elder adult may end up as a sole caregiver for one parent after the other has passed away. Too often, because the disease was not revealed, they are shocked to find that Mom or Dad is no longer safe being left alone and are forced to find solutions within a very short period of time.

In these instances, it is important to know about and understand the resources available, to help research and educate people put in these difficult positions. Care managers, professional guardians, and social workers are all good sources for information. These professionals use the combined knowledge of health needs, human development, family dynamics, and public and private resources, as well as funding sources, costs, quality, and availability of services in their communities to make recommendations for those seeking advice. Elder law attorneys have expertise in available financial planning alternatives, and can help make sense of the different care options and the viability of each choice while considering individual dynamics within differing family circumstances.

Becoming as educated and prepared as possible prior to making an important decision regarding the care of your loved one can make the process less daunting. Having a plan, narrowing search options, and utilizing available resources can all serve as tools for making the choices that are right for your family and your specific circumstances.

Reach out, study the Internet, visit support groups, talk to friends, connect with the Alzheimer's Association. It's a lot of homework but well worth your time in the long run.

Resources
Caring.com: Is a memory care unit or a nursing home better?: http://bit.ly/1OVcq5c
AgingCare.com E-book: Facing Alzheimer's with Strength and Grace: http://bit.ly/1OTDYJU
Healthline.com: Disease Progression—The 5 Stages of Dementia: www.healthline.com/health/dementia/stages
Examiner.com: Is It Time to Move Your Loved One to a Memory Care Home?: http://exm.nr/1IHgkyZ

*Rebecca Weitzel is certified by the Alzheimer's Association as a support group facilitator and by the State of Florida in Assisted Living Core Training and Extended Congregate Care, and provides educational seminars nationwide. She is currently obtaining her Ph.D. in Gerontology, and continues to work with caregivers and their loved ones in need of information, support, or an empathetic listener. For more information visit info@RebeccaWeitzel.com*

*Dale Griffen*

## What Does That Mean? A Guide to Caregiving Terms

We now live in the information age, with access to information as close as your cell phone or computer. However, sometimes when healthcare providers communicate, they use words, acronyms, and terms that seem foreign and confusing. Part of what we do at The Go! Agency every day is foster on-line connections and relationships between healthcare providers, patients and clients, and referral sources through the use of social media. We strongly suggest you research your providers on-line, write down as much as you can at appointments, and search out topics that you don't fully understand. Use search engines such as Google. Do topic searches on Facebook and Twitter (using hashtags) to get the exact information you're looking for (such as #caregiverstress or #diabeticdiet) and be sure to consult with your physician on any decisions or new ideas you may find.

To help you navigate through the sometimes-confusing jargon—the healthcare field loves to create acronyms—at your next doctor's appointment, this information is divided into two sections of caregiving terms: Acronyms and a Glossary.

### Acronyms

**ADL:** Activities of Daily Living

**ADR:** Adverse Drug Reaction

**ALF**: Assisted Living Facility

**ADRC**: Aging and Disability Resource Center

**ALF**: Assisted Living Facility

**AOA**: U.S. Dept. of Health & Human Services Administration on Aging

**ARCH**: Adult Residential Care Home

**CCRC**: Continuing Care Retirement Community

**CMO**: Comfort Measures Only

**CNA**: Certified Nursing Assistant

**CPR**: Cardiopulmonary Resuscitation

**CVA**: Stroke (also: Cerebrovascular Accident)

**DNR**: Do Not Resuscitate order

**DME**: Durable Medical Equipment

**DPOAHC**: Durable Power of Attorney for Health Care

**ECC**: Extended Congregate Care License

**FMLA**: Family and Medical Leave Act

**HCFA**: Health Care Financing Administration

**HHA**: Home Health Aide

**HIPAA**: Health Insurance Portability and Accountability Act

**HMO**: Health Maintenance Organization

**ILF**: Independent Living Facility

**LMH**: Limited Mental Health License

**LNS**: Limited Nursing Services License

**LTC**: Long-Term Care

**OT**: Occupational Therapist

**OTA**: Occupational Therapy Assistant

**PCP**: Primary Care Physician

**POA**: Power of Attorney

**PPO**: Preferred Provider Organization

**PT**: Physical Therapist

**PTA**: Physical Therapy Assistant

**SLP**: Speech-Language Pathologist (also: Speech Therapist)

**SLPA**: Speech-Language Pathology Assistant

**SNF**: Skilled Nursing Facility

**SSI**: Supplemental Security Income Program

**UTI**: Urinary Tract Infection


## Glossary of Caregiving Terms

**AARP**—Formerly the American Association of Retired Persons, a non-profit advocate membership organization for people age fifty and over. One of the most powerful lobbying groups in the United States.

**Accelerated Death Benefit**—Many life insurance policies allow a person to receive a portion of their life insurance money early, to use while they are still alive.

**Activities of Daily Living** (ADL)—Basic activities a person performs each day, such as dressing, grooming, bathing, toileting, etc.

**Acute Care**—Immediate care, often in the hospital setting.

**Acute Illness/Pain**—A condition that is severe and has a sudden onset. See Chronic Illness/Pain

**Adult Residential Care Home** (ARCH)—For semi-independent residents in need of assistance with ADLs. Type I: facility with five or fewer residents, family home setting. Type II: fifty or more residents, institutional setting.

**Adult Day Care/Services**—An organized, supervised day program that offers activities, socialization, and personal services, allowing caregivers respite.

**Adult Family Care Home**—A residential home that provides personal care to individuals requiring assistance. The provider must live in the home and may accommodate up to five residents.

**Adult Protective Services**—An agency that protects vulnerable adults from abuse, neglect, exploitation, or self-neglect, it also enables adults with disabilities to remain in the community.

**Advanced Directive**—Instruction for others regarding future needs. See Health Care Surrogate, Power of Attorney, Living Will

**Advance Directive for Health Care**—See Living Will

**Adverse Drug Reaction** (ADR)—An injury caused by taking a medication(s).

**Alzheimer's Disease**—See Dementia

Ambulatory—Able to walk, and not bedridden.

**Assisted Living Facility** (ALF)—Long-term housing that provides personal care and services such as meals, medication management, bathing, dressing, and transportation.

**Beneficiary**—A person designated as the recipient of funds, a will or trust, or life insurance.

**Burnout**—Mental or physical breakdown caused by overwork or stress.

**Caregiver**—A person who regularly looks after a sick, elderly, or disabled person.

**Care Manager/Case Manager**—One who assists, identifies, and coordinates services needed.

**Certified Nursing Assistant (CNA)**—A state-licensed individual with special training who assists and reports to RNs and LPNs in basic patient care, and assists patients with their needs.

**Cerebrovascular Accident (CVA)**—See Stroke

**Chronic Illness/Pain**—A condition that is persists for a long time or recurs constantly. See Acute Illness/Pain

**Codicil**—An addition, supplement, or change that modifies, alters, or revokes a will or part of a will.

**Coinsurance**—Your share of the costs of a covered healthcare service. You pay this after you've met your deductible.

**Companionship Services**—A non-medical caregiver who provides in-home companionship, and keeps a loved one socially engaged, can accompany them to visit friends, family, and other social events.

**Conservator(ship)**—A guardian and protector appointed by the court to protect and manage the financial affairs and/or the person's daily life.

**Continence**—Control of bowel and/or bladder.

**Continuing Care Retirement Community (CCRC)**—These facilities have independent living, assisted living, and license nursing services under one roof, which allows transition through care without requiring residents to move as their conditions change.

**Continuum of Care**—The array of health services spanning all levels and intensity of care.

**Contraindications**—A drug, procedure, or surgery that may be harmful to the person.

**Coordination of Benefits**—Helps ensure that members covered by more than one plan will receive the benefits they are entitled to, while avoiding overpayment by either plan.

**Co-payment**—A specified amount of out-of-pocket expenses for healthcare services.

**Coping (Skills)**—Ways we deal with various stresses. These differ for each person.

**Corticosteroids**—Steroid hormones, usually used to treat inflammation.

**Deductible**—A specific amount of money that must be paid before an insurance company will pay a claim.

**Dementia**—A mental disorder where brain disease or injury may cause impaired memory, reasoning, and/or personality changes.

**Dementia Tour**—A kit used to simulate the symptoms of Alzheimer's and dementia that helps caregivers better understand their patients' behaviors and needs.

**Depression**—A mood disorder that causes a feeling of sadness and loss of interest.

**Discharge Planner**—One who coordinates what a patient needs for a smooth move from one level of care to another.

**Do Not Resuscitate Order (DNR)**—This form alerts emergency personnel that the individual does not wish to receive cardiopulmonary resuscitation (CPR).

**Durable Medical Equipment (DME)**—Equipment that assists a patient in need, due to certain medical conditions and/or illnesses.

**Durable Power of Attorney**—See Power of Attorney

**Durable Power of Attorney for Health Care (DPOAHC)**—See Power of Attorney for Health Care

**Hospice**—Multi-disciplinary care, in-home or at a facility, that supports the patient and family in end-of-life care, pain relief, spiritual care, quality of life, and bereavement.

**Elder Attorney**—See Elder Law

**Elder Law**—An area of legal practice focusing on issues that affect the aging population.

**End-of-Life Care**—Specific care of those with a terminal illness, disease, or condition.

**Enteral Nutrition**—Use of tubes to administer fluids, nutrients, and more into the digestive tract.

**Estate Planning**—Preparing pre-death directives related to a person's assets, finances, insurance, and debt.

**Executor**—The person or entity appointed to carry out the terms of one's will.

**Extended Congregate Care License (ECC)**—An assisted living facility with an ECC license allows a resident to age in place by providing the basic services of an assisted living facility, as well as limited nursing services and assessments; total help with bathing, dressing, grooming, and toileting; measurement and recording of vital signs and weight; dietary management, including special diets, monitoring nutrition, food, and fluid intake; supervising residents with dementia and/or cognitive impairments; providing or arranging for rehabilitative services; providing escort services to medical appointments; and educational programs to promote health and prevent illness.

**Family and Medical Leave Act (FMLA)**—A U.S. federal law that allows employees job protection and unpaid leave for qualified medical and family reasons.

**Geriatric Care Manager**—One who specializes in gerontology, social work, or nursing. See Care Manager

**Guardian(ship)**—One who cares for and maintains legal responsibility for a person (a ward) deemed unable to care for him- or herself.

**Health Care Directive**—See Living Will

**Health Care Proxy**—Document that appoints someone to make healthcare decisions if the person has not selected a Health Care Surrogate prior to becoming unable to make these decisions on his or her own.

**Health Care Surrogate**—Someone you select to make healthcare decisions for you, if and when you become unable to do so yourself. Appointing a Power of Attorney ahead of time allows you to choose who this person is.

**Health Insurance Portability and Accountability Act (HIPAA)**—Federal laws protecting patient privacy.

**Health Maintenance Organization (HMO)**—Insurance plan that grants access to certain doctors and hospitals within its network. An HMO may be more affordable than a PPO, but may offer less coverage and more restrictions. Also see PPO

**Home Health/Home Care**—Services that allow people to stay in their dwellings, by providing intermittent care, ADLs, medical care and supervision, companionship, rehabilitation, etc.

**Home Health**—Therapy, nursing, medications, injections, wound care, medical tests, monitoring of health status, etc.

**Home Care**—ADLs, meal prep, companionship, transportation, etc.

**Home Health Aide (HHA)**—A nurse's aide specialized in working in the home. See CNA

**Hospice**—An organization that specializes in the care of people who are terminally ill. The focus is on compassionate emotional and spiritual care for both patient and family.

**Hyper/Hypo**—Hyper means more than normal; hypo means less than normal.

**Hyperglycemia/Hypoglycemia**—High or low blood sugar.

**Hypertension/Hypo-tension**—Pertaining to high or low blood pressure.

**Incontinence**—Inability to control bowel or bladder function.

**Independent Living Facility** (ILF)—Communities designed for those over aged fifty-five, with amenities, activities, and services designed for aging adults. Many facilities offer the ability to "age in place" with assisted living and skilled nursing units on site. Also known as retirement communities, senior living communities, or independent retirement communities.

**Informed Consent**—A written agreement a patient signs to give permission for a medical procedure (such as surgery) after having been informed of potential risks, benefits, and side effects.

**Intermediate Care**—The time between dependence and independence, typically after hospitalization and before the individual has sufficiently recovered to resume self-care.

**Irrevocable Trust**—A legal arrangement that cannot be changed by the grantor. It is the opposite of a revocable trust, which allows the grantor to change the terms of the trust at any time.

**Journaling**—Keeping a written history of one's thoughts and feelings surrounding certain events in one's life. Journaling is often used as a stress management and self-exploration tool.

**Life Care Plan**—Plans and documents generally formulated with an elder law attorney, which help families and seniors respond to perceivable challenges that might be caused by chronic illness or disability.

**Limited Nursing Services License (LNS)**—An assisted living facility with an LNS license provides the basic services of an ALF as well as specific nursing services. Some of the limited nursing services are: nursing assessments; care and application of routine dressings; care of casts, braces, and splints; administration and regulation of portable oxygen; catheter, colostomy, and ileostomy care and maintenance; application of cold or heat treatments; passive range-of-motion exercises; ear and eye irrigations; and other services as defined in law.

**Limited Mental Health License (LMH)**—A license required if an ALF serves three or more mental health residents. Services must be provided for the special needs of these residents, along with the basic services of an ALF. A facility with this license must consult with the resident and the resident's mental health case manager to develop and carry out a community living support plan.

**Living Trust**—When one person (the trustee) is in legal possession of assets that belong to another (the beneficiary) while still alive.

**Living Will**—Part of a Health Care Directive or declaration, also known as a personal directive, advance directive, or advance decision, in which a person puts in writing what they do and do not want in terms of medical care if ever unable to speak for themselves. A Living Will includes your wishes regarding any life-prolonging measures.

**Long-Term Care Facility (LTC)**—A facility for people who require help with their physical or emotional needs over an extended period of time.

**Long-Term Care Insurance**—Coverage for care at a nursing home, with home health, or adult day-care for individuals sixty-five or older who have a chronic condition.

**Long-Term Care Ombudsman**—Someone to advocate on a resident's behalf to resolve problems, address issues, or work to change systemic problems.

**Managed Care**—A system of health care in which treatment is monitored by a managing company in an effort to reduce costs while improving the quality of care.

**Medicaid**—Federally funded, state-run program for qualifying low-income people, to help pay for certain medical care.

**Medicare**—The federal health insurance program for individuals sixty-five or older, and others with certain disabilities.

**Medicare Supplement Insurance**—An insurance program that may fill in "gaps" between what is covered by Medicare Part A (hospital insurance) and Part B (medical insurance). Items that may be covered include deductibles, co-payments, and other expenses.

**Medigap Insurance**—See Medicare Supplement Insurance

**Memory Care**—Care for those with Alzheimer's or dementia, which is provided in a secure, sometimes separate part of a facility. Accommodations may range from semi-private apartments to private rooms. Structured activities are delivered by trained staff members.

**Nursing Home**—Residential accommodations with trained and/or licensed staff to provide healthcare, personal care, and therapies for elderly and/or disabled people. Nursing homes are not covered by Medicare, as a SNF is. Other names: convalescent home, skilled nursing facility (SNF), care home, rest home, or intermediate care.

**Occupational Therapist (OT)**—A licensed professional who helps people improve their ability to perform tasks of daily living. Occupational Therapy Assistants (OTAs) may work under the direction and supervision of Occupational Therapists.

**Ombudsman**—A person appointed to investigate complaints of public authorities.

**Osteoarthritis**—Degenerative disease of joint cartilage and underlying bone.

**Palliative Care** (Pain Relief)—Care given when death is desired to occur naturally without life-prolonging intervention, other than pain relief and CMO (Comfort Measures Only).

**Personal Care**—See Activities of Daily Living

**Physical Therapist**—A licensed professional who help patients reduce pain and/or improve and/or restore mobility. Physical Therapy Assistants (PTAs) may work under the direction and supervision of Physical Therapists.

**Power of Attorney** (POA)—A durable power of attorney for health care names someone as your healthcare agent to oversee your financial and health care wishes and make any necessary decisions for you.

**Preferred Provider Organization** (PPO)—An insurance plan that is more flexible and provides greater coverage and provider choices than an HMO, but is more costly and may have greater deductibles.

**Primary Care Physician** (PCP)—A practitioner or internist who provides initial and long-term care, and treats many health issues. A PCP may refer a patient to specialists as needed.

**Primary Caregiver**—A family member, a trained professional or other individual who takes responsibility for a person who cannot care for him- or herself.

**Rehabilitation**—Treatment that aids in the process of recovery from injury, illness, or disease, back to as normal a state as possible.

**Reluctant Caregiver**—One who must take on the role of caring for an individual because of the situation. This can be very difficult, mentally or physically uncomfortable, and may incur resentment as it takes them away from their own responsibilities.

**Respite Care**—Temporary care of a dependent person, whereby relief is provided for the primary caregiver. This care can be paid or unpaid, in an institution, or in the home.

**Revocable Trust**—A trust that can be altered or canceled by the grantor (the person who makes the trust). While the grantor is alive, income earned is distributed to them; after death the property transfers to any beneficiaries.

**Sandwich Generation**—People, typically between their thirties and fifties, who are simultaneously responsible for bringing up their own children and caring for their aging parents.

**Self-Care**—Intentional actions one takes to care for his or her own physical, mental, and emotional health needs.

**Side Effects**—A peripheral or secondary response, usually unintended and undesirable, to a drug or therapy.

**Senior Center**—A type of community center for older adults to engage in a variety of social, physical, emotional, and intellectual activities. Many are locally funded and some receive state and federal funding.

**Skilled Care**—Nursing and/or rehabilitation care, management, observation, and evaluation in the heathcare continuum, including nursing as well as physical, occupational, and speech therapy.

**Skilled Nursing Facility (SNF)**—A Medicare-covered facility with trained and/or licensed staff that provides healthcare, personal care, and therapies for the elderly and/or disabled, or recovering patients, for a temporary period of time.

**Social Security**—A federal government insurance system that provides financial assistance for those with low or no income, retired people, and those who are unemployed or disabled. Programs run by Social Security are Supplemental Security Income (SSI) and Social Security Disability Income (SSDI).

**Speech Therapist**—Also called a Speech-Language Pathologist (SLP), a licensed professional who treats people with speech defects or disorders, utilizing exercises and new speech habits. Speech-Language Pathology Assistants (SLPAs) may work under the direction and supervision of Speech Therapists.

**Stroke**—When blood flow fails to reach the brain due to blockage or rupture of an artery, causing brain cells to die quickly due to lack of oxygen. Symptoms may be slurred or sudden loss of speech, weakness, or paralysis of one side of the body. Also known as Cerebrovascular Accident, or CVA.

**Sub-Acute Care**—In-patient care for patients who are medically stable and no longer require acute hospital care.

**Support Group**—A group of people with common experiences or concerns. Many times moderated by a facilitator, these groups provide encouragement, comfort, and advice.

**Surrogate**—See Health Care Surrogate

**Term Life Insurance**—Life insurance that pays a benefit in the event of the death of the insured during a specified time period, or "term."

**Trust**—A legal arrangement that allows a third party to hold assets on behalf of the beneficiary. Trusts can be arranged in many ways and can specify exactly how and when the assets pass to the beneficiaries.

**Trustee**—A person or entity with control over a trust, with the ability to administer it as specified.

**Universal Life Insurance**—A life insurance policy that provides the flexibility to build the policy's cash value or focus more on guaranteed protection.

**Veterans Benefits**—Health and other benefits based on one's military service. Contact the U.S. Department of Veterans Affairs.

**Will**—Also called a "Last Will and Testament," a document that outlines one's final wishes. The will is read after death, and the court makes sure that the deceased's final wishes are carried out.

**Whole Life Insurance**—A form of permanent life insurance, whole life insurance features guaranteed premiums, death benefits, and cash value. Policies also provide the potential to receive dividends, which can increase the value of the policy when the insured is living, or provide an increased death benefit for beneficiaries.

*Dale Griffen is vice president of the on-line marketing firm The Go! Agency. A registered nurse with more than twenty years experience in the medical arena, he oversees the agency's healthcare marketing team and is author of* The Secrets to Healthcare Marketing. *For more information visit www.thegoagencyusa.com*

## Website Resources

*Please note: Long website addresses have been shortened to permanent links for your ease in reaching the informational sites.*

### Public Agencies

Administration on Aging: www.aoa.gov

AgingCare.com: www.agingcare.com

End of Life: Helping With Comfort and Care:
www.1.usa.gov/1QSuXkU

Family Caregiver Alliance: www.caregiver.org

Healthline: www.healthline.com

FHA-Insured Reverse Mortgage:
www.1.usa.gov/18mjQay

National Institute on Aging: www.nia.nih.gov

National Institute on Aging: Alzheimer's:
www.nia.nih.gov/alzheimers

National Institute of Health: www.nih.gov

National Institute of Health: Neurological Disorders &
Stroke: www.1.usa.gov/23BcLEx

U.S. Dept. of Veterans Affairs: www.va.gov

Veteran Benfits Info:
www.benefits.va.gov/BENEFITS/factsheets.asp

VA Caregiver Support: www.caregiver.va.gov
**Private Sites, Organizations and Foundations**

AARP: www.aarp.org

Aging Life Care Association: www.aginglifecare.org

Alzheimer's Association: www.alz.org

Alzheimer's Disease Education and Referral Center:
www.nia.nih.gov/alzheimers

Alzheimer's Foundation of America: www.alzfdn.org

Alzheimer's Research & Prevention Foundation—
www.alzheimersprevention.org

American Legion: www.legion.org

Assisted Living Today: www.assistedlivingtoday.com

Better Business Bureau: www.bbb.org

Case Management Society of America: www.cmsa.org

Caring.com: Find Senior Living: www.caring.com

Center for Loss & Life Transition—
www.centerforloss.com

The Eden Alternative: www.edenalt.org

Family Caregiver Alliance: www.caregiver.org

Florida Caregivers Network:
www.floridacaregiversnetwork.org

Make the Connection: Videos & Info for Military
Veterans: www.maketheconnection.net

Memory Bridge: www.memorybridge.org

Military and Veteran Benefits: www.military.com

National Aging in Place Council: www.ageinplace.org

National Assoc. of County Veteran Service Officers:

www.nacvso.org

National Center for Creative Aging:
   www.creativeaging.org

National Council on Aging: www.ncoa.org/

National Mortgage Licensing System: bit.ly/1AFoeBf

National Reverse Mortgage Lenders Association:
   www.reversemortgage.org

Pioneer Network: www.pioneernetwork.net

Purple Cities Alliance: www.facebook.com/purplecities/

Veterans Crisis Line (1-800-273-TALK):
   www.veteranscrisisline.net


## Books & Periodicals

The 36-hour Day: A Family Guide to Caring for People With Alzheimer's Disease, Other Dementias, and Memory Loss in Later Life: amzn.to/1RLZP2Z

The Alzheimer's Action Plan: The Experts' Guide to the Best Diagnosis and Treatment for Memory Problems: amzn.to/1UwDJqb

Alzheimer's Early Stages: First Steps for Family, Friends and Caregivers: amzn.to/1RM4AcW

Caregiver Stress: Neurobiology to the Rescue: amzn.to/20stzqs

Disease Progression—The 5 Stages of Dementia: bit.ly/1qrEfnV

Facing Alzheimer's with Strength and Grace: bit.ly/1OTDYJU

The Forgetting. Alzheimer's: Portrait of an Epidemic:
    amzn.to/1prN5bB

Is a memory care unit or a nursing home better:
    bit.ly/1OVcq5c

Is It Time to Move Your Loved One to a Memory Care
    Home: exm.nr/1IHgkyZ

Mayo Clinic Guide to Alzheimer's Disease: The
    Essential Resource for Treatment, Coping and
    Caregiving: amzn.to/1LoO2Lk

Music and Memory: Elders with Dementia Find Hope
    in a Song, Social Work Today: bit.ly/2207TV2

A Review of Social Isolation, by Nicholas R.
    Nicholson; The Journal of Primary Prevention:
    1.usa.gov/1SWLBQk

New York Times: Alzheimer's Disease News & Features:
    nyti.ms/1U0WVOr

Virginia Bell and Davie Troxel's Best Friends™ Approach to
    Alzheimer's Care: http://amzn.to/1TQp8EF


### Miscellaneous

Good Old Days: www.goodolddaysmagazine.com

LinkedSenior: 6 Health Benefits of Having Hobbies &
    Leisure Activities: bit.ly/1LE1gCp

Old Radio World: bit.ly/1U4FOv5

Reminisce magazine: www.reminisce.com

RadioLovers Old Time Radio Shows:
    www.radiolovers.com

## Contributor Sites

Jonathan Bowman, Harmony Home Health:
www.harmonyhh.com

Linda Burhans, Linda's Caregiver Connections:
www.lindascaregiverconnections.com

Mel Coppola, Hearts in Care:
www.heartsincare.com

Heidi Crockett:
www.HeidiCrockett.com

Mary Jane Cronin, Cronin Counseling:
www.cronincounseling.com

Stephanie M. Edwards, Edwards Elder Law, P.A:
www.edwardselderlaw.com

Linda Freed, Wishes 4 Wellness Nursing Care
Management: www.Wishes4Wellness.com

Candy Goodwin, CLTC, Vernick Financial Planning:
www.vernickfinancial.com

Dale Griffen, The Go! Agency:
www.thegoagencyusa.com

Karen Karle-Truman, Ph.D., Dementia Caregiver
Resources, Inc.: www.dcrinc.org

Gary Joseph LeBlanc, Common Sense Caregiving:
www.commonsensecaregiving.com

Karyn Rizzo, Elite Marketing & Consulting:
www.agingguidebook1.com

Paula Stahel, Breath & Shadows Productions:
    www.breathandshadows.com

Malcolm Tennant, Access Reverse Mortgage Corp:
    www.accessreversemortgage.com

Marieke Van Donkersgoed, Cypress Healing:
    www.cypresshealing.com

Maria Winer, Maria's Adult Day Care:
    www.mariacares.com